The author, 1972

Stanley A W Gyles has been in the printing and graphic arts industry most of his life and has been an accomplished copywriter and journalist for more than 20 years before forming his own marketing and advertising agency. As a journalist he has covered sport in Australia, New Zealand, UK and Asia. He has a fond love of wine, food, music and travel and all sports, in particular, rugby union, cricket, sailing and golf. This is his second book. He lives in Melbourne, Australia.

In memory of and dedicated to:

Edward (Kiwi Ted) Holmes

Quentin (Anchor) Ryan

Stanley A W Gyles

THE SINKING OF THE ANTIPODEAN

AUSTIN MACAULEY PUBLISHERS™

LONDON • CAMBRIDGE • NEW YORK • SHARJAH

A CIP catalogue record for this title is available from the British Library.

ISBN 9781788789028 (Paperback)
ISBN 9781788789035 (Hardback)
ISBN 9781528956338 (ePub e-book)

www.austinmacauley.com

First Published (2020)
Austin Macauley Publishers Ltd
25 Canada Square
Canary Wharf
London
E14 5LQ

I am grateful to the crew and all those associated with the Antipodean. It's obvious to say that without them this book would not be possible.

Voyages of the "ANTIPODEAN"
1973-1974

The journey of the Antipodean

Cover Design and Graphics
Rod Attenborough
www.rodatt.com

"I think this is it!"

The storm had been building up for days; now the waves had grown to tower over the small boat.

"The yacht's beginning to disintegrate and I'm bloody scared," screamed Roscoe, clinging to the guardrail.

Lightening flashed across the blackened sky. A gale force wind blew filling the air with foam and spray. The sea crested with white froth. Waves crashed down, cascading over and swamping the yacht. The driving spray blinded the occupants as they attempted to steer the boat. Tossing aimlessly, the *Antipodean* twisted and turned, completely out of control.

It was just before 0700hrs on 22 October 1974.

"Batten down the hatches," screamed Kaffir.

The five sailors on board panicked as the waves continued to pound their tiny yacht. The foaming water found every crack and gushed into the cabin.

"Shit, what can we do?" yelled Peter. They looked at each other, holding onto anything solid for support. The sodden weary crew members, bleary eyed from the lack of sleep for more than 30 hours looked a forlorn sight. The silence between them was only broken by the sound of the boat groaning and creaking in the torturous seas. The howling wind and continuous claps of thunder echoed in their ears. They were desperate.

"Jesus, I think this is the end," screamed Anchor, into the howling wind.

"Crap! We can beat this," yelled Kaffir.

"Okay, smart arse, how?"

"Look, the depth sounder says we're in about 60 feet. We're about half a mile from the coast and it's getting no closer. I reckon if we get all our anchor chain and rope over the side, it might stabilise us a bit."

They all looked at each other. The situation was grim.

"Sam, Roscoe and Anchor, you stay in the cabin and pray. Peter, you and I will go on deck and try and let the anchor down," ordered Kaffir.

"Are you up to it?"

"Sort of," was Peter's apprehensive reply.

The two of them clambered through the cabin and as they huddled in the cockpit took stock of the situation. Kaffir was wearing his life possessions: two T-shirts, a woollen jumper, two faded rugby jerseys and a long greatcoat. Peter was clad in three heavy jumpers and was wearing a tattered pair of shorts.

Antipodean was now side on to the waves.

"The chains are in the aft hatch," yelled Kaffir, scrambling across the deck. They prised the hatch off and with his head buried inside; Kaffir began feeding the heavy main anchor chain out. Above him, grasping his shoulders, Peter fed the first six feet of chain onto the deck. In these conditions, it was hard work and progress was slow. Then it happened! Calmly, Peter tapped Kaffir on the shoulder, "Have a look at this."

About 50 feet away, a huge white wave was coming. It was curling above them, ready to smash down on *Antipodean*. Behind it, another wave loomed. They had only a moment to grab something. Instinctively, the two of them ran, stumbling across the deck. Peter to the main mast wrapping his legs around its base, his hands grasping each other as he struggled to hold on. Kaffir ran to the shrouds and hung onto the chain plates.

Meanwhile, Roscoe had been crouching in the cockpit watching the two of them work furiously on the anchor chain. His face dropped when he saw the two waves approaching. Turning, he jumped into the cabin.

"Shit, hang on. This is it. A big one's coming!" Sam braced himself for the hit.

"Where's Anchor?" he screamed, his voice almost inaudible.

"He's in the shit house."

"Oh no, you must be joking."

The wave struck sending Kaffir sprawling across the deck, his arms flailing trying to grab some sort of support. Peter retained his grip on the mast and looked helplessly on as Kaffir slid and rolled across the deck struggling to get to his feet. In the relative safety of the cabin, Sam and Roscoe grabbed the bunks and held on grimly as water gushed in swamping them.

"Are you OK, Roscoe?" Sam nervously yelled.

"Yeah, but I don't know about Anchor."

In the small confines of the yacht's tiny toilet he was thrown backwards and with his trousers around his ankles wasn't able to move.

"I'm trapped," he yelled.

At that moment, Roscoe had crawled out of the cabin and was again surveying things from the cockpit. It wasn't nice and he gulped nervously watching Kaffir and Peter through the spray. Kaffir looked up, terrified. The second wave, bigger than the first, was about to smash down on them. It suddenly hit with ferocious power, striking Kaffir in the chest, washing him overboard into the depths of the Mediterranean Sea.

In an instance, Peter met the same fate and followed his captain overboard. The wave and current dragged him downward.

Roscoe screamed into the cabin 'Mayday, Mayday!' It was chaos. The boat flipped over like a gymnast doing a tumbling roll. With the pressure of the impact, the mast snapped. There was a deafening sound of something smashing up. The bunks and galley had disintegrated.

"Oh God, this is it," cried Roscoe with tears welling in his eyes.

The panelling broke up, a piece jagging into Sam's head. He was stunned and was struggling to determine his next move. Roscoe had been flung to the floor of the cabin, his face submerged in the water. Spluttering and gulping for air, he regained his feet.

In the loo, Anchor had been flipped upright, cracking his head on the bowl of the toilet. His backside was severely bruised and with his trousers still around his ankles, his movements were restricted. Everything momentarily was in darkness.

Suddenly the boat flipped upright and there was daylight.

"Shit, the cabin top from the deck has gone. That's a big fucking hole," Sam yelled to Roscoe. "It's broken away from the hull. We'll have to swim for our lives."

"Let's go," he yelled.

They had no choice. Another wave struck sending the two of them hurtling into the ocean. This wave sent Anchor crashing into the shattered toilet wall as he continued to wrestle off his trousers. By now water was waist deep and it seemed to be the end for him. His whole body was bruised, his head was bloody and his genitals were numb. A fourth wave hit what was left of the floating wreck.

Anchor had no say in his fate. The waves whisked him out of the super structure into the sea.

It was August 1972.

Brian (Kaffir) Muir and his New Zealand mate, Mike Anderson, were lazing on a beach in front of the 'La Ballena Alegre' camping ground, north of Barcelona in Spain gazing out to sea. Moored 200 feet or so off shore was a flotilla of small fishing boats, yachts and a couple of catamarans.

Girls in very small, tight bikinis caught their eye. Walking or sunbathing on the beach were mostly tourists relaxing during their summer vacation.

The boys were relaxed. And no wonder.

They had just arrived after a voyage from Cape Town to Lisbon on board a rusty Portuguese passenger liner. From Lisbon they had driven to Barcelona in the cheapest rental car that they could hire.

"Let's steal a boat and sail it back to Australia," Kaffir, suddenly blurted out.

An Aussie they had met at the camping ground joined them. His name was Kenny 'Nice Guy' Smith. Why 'Nice Guy'? Well, that's what the girls called him – a nice guy!

A product of James Cook High School in the Sydney, suburb of Kogarah, Kenny had a poor academic record but learnt more after he left school and took up a five-year apprenticeship as a toolmaker. Within weeks of finishing his time, he was surfing the huge waves of Cape St Francis, on a headland in the eastern province of South Africa. The location had been made famous by the legendry film maker Bruce Brown, in the 1966 cult surfing movie 'The Endless Summer'.

After nine months in Durban and a stint in Cape Town, Kenny eventually found his way to Andorra and from there, hitch hiked to the Barcelona camping ground. He was certainly better groomed with short back and sides and better behaved than the crew that would be eventually assembled for the proposed Trans – Pacific voyage.

"Hey, Kenny, we're thinking of nicking a boat and sailing it back to Oz. Will you be in it?" asked Mike.

"Shit, guys, that's a big call. Where are you going to find a boat like that? Australia is a bloody long way."

"Yeah, but look at all those boats bobbing up and down," said Kaffir pointing out into the bay. "Nobody's using them and nobody wants them."

"Yeah, but I reckon we'll need a solid sort of clinker built boat that will withstand storms and stuff," said Mike.

"Too slow! That big cat over there will zoom over the waves. No one will catch us in that," Kaffir said, eyeing a couple of girls who were shedding their bikini tops nearby.

The boys paused, watching the girls smother oil over each other's breasts before lying down face up to the sun.

"I'm quite comfortable here actually. The scenery's pretty good and I know where their camp site is," said Mike, propping himself up for a better view.

"I wouldn't steal anything in Spain," said Kenny changing the subject, "Franco is in power and if we get caught, then its jail for sure."

Kenny had the last say on the subject. But the idea had been born – to sail a boat from London to Sydney and then New Zealand.

Kaffir got his nickname after spending eighteen months bumming around Central Africa, picking up work as an itinerant chippie. The name fitted and stuck. He was born in the one pub town of Raetihi, in an area known as the King Country in New Zealand. The son of a grocer, the family moved to Napier when he was ten years old. He was a poor scholar, achieving very little at school.

When he was 14, he joined the Napier Sailing Club where he learnt the skills and gained the confidence to be able to take on such a foolhardy voyage as the one you are about to read. Sitting on this far away beach, he was scruffy and unshaven with long unkempt black hair and a Mexican Zapata moustache. His appearance never changed over the following few years. Always stony broke, his clothes fitted comfortably into a little old Air New Zealand travel bag. He always wore a pair of Kaffatakkies – sandals made out of old recycled car tyres, as worn by the native South Africans.

Mike, also a carpenter could be confused with Jesus Christ – not just by trade. He had the same dark hair, the same beard and had a spiritual air about him. Born in New Zealand and brought up in the Bay of Plenty, he had an enquiring mind. He was a thinker with an eye for detail with a softly spoken drawl. He loved to have a long and meaningful conversation – unusual characteristics for a carpenter you might think.

The campsite was full of backpackers and before long our travellers talked their way into sharing a ride in an old 1960's Kombi van to London.

"Our contribution will be a 25 litre plastic container of Castilla La Mancha red wine," said Kaffir.

"Shit Kaf, that's generous," said Kenny.

"It's the cheapest plonk in Spain. Wait till you experience a hangover on it."

Progress was slow as the van headed towards Calais, destination Dover. There were long periods of boredom.

"Give 'em a brown eye," the driver said.

"What's that?" asked Kenny.

"Drop your trousers and press your bare bum against the back window,"

"OK," said Kenny who then took great delight in scaring impatient motorists following the slow van.

Shortly after, the idea of sailing across the world was on the boil again. Kenny temporally went to Canada to seek his fortune. After the trip from South Africa and the brief sojourn in Spain, Mike and Kaffir needed money urgently to survive in London and to finance their unique lifestyle of beer and women.

They gratefully accepted an offer to work on a building site near Buckingham Palace. But these were days of union unrest and they could not start because the site was picketed. Instead many idle hours were spent in numerous pubs or flicking through copies of Exchange and Mart and the many other sailing magazines.

Residence in London was at 16 Woodland Gardens, Muswell Hill which was near Highgate Tube Station on the Northern underground line. It was a typical London two storey terrace brick house consisting a small back yard with its frontage on the street. It had been converted into three bedsits upstairs and a three bedroom flat downstairs.

There was also a small kitchen with a broken window, the legacy of an empty 'Watney's Party Seven' beer can used as a football during one of the many daily parties that occupied the lifestyle of the day. The window remained broken all winter.

The house was shabby inside. Rising damp had caused plaster and tiles to crack or fall off the walls in the kitchen and shower. A stench of stale beer and cheap perfume always hung in the air.

Dirty washing lay all over the place and the smell of body odour was continually present. Visitors of both sexes regularly came and went. Sleeping on the floor after missing the last tube home was a regular occurrence.

It became a doss house for Aussies and Kiwis going to, or returning from Europe. There wasn't any hot water downstairs, due to an on-going dispute with the gas company. Something about, "we paid the account."

"No, you didn't."

"Yes, we did."

However, upstairs the hot water was coin operated and mysteriously the padlock had fallen off, allowing the same 20 pence piece to be endlessly recycled. Everyone except the gas company was happy.

The dispute was never resolved.

The bedsits upstairs were occupied by some Aussie girls while Kaffir had a small space on the lounge floor below to call his own. The key housemates were Mike, Kenny and two others, who were invited to join the sailing project, Sam Syme and Ted 'The Dart' Gregorski.

Sam was short, nuggetty, barrel chested, a fanatical surfer and a former first-grade rugby union player with the Port Hacking Rugby Club in Sydney. His short tight curly blond hair was above a ginger beard. He was easy going without a care and was often seen naked, showing off what was reputed to be the smallest penis in the world.

In total contrast, Ted 'The Dart' was tall, gangly, short sighted and clumsy. He did, however make the first 18 Aussie Rules team as a ruckman at Christian Brothers School in Albany, NSW. Ted had more brains than the others and was a top five HSC student at the well-known respected catholic school. But things went horribly wrong when he left school and began training at the Manly Seminary as a Catholic Priest. He lasted one week!

He completely changed direction and took employment as an admin officer in Canberra so he could study part time for a degree in economics at The Australian National University. Three years later and very much in love, Ted followed his girlfriend to Johannesburg, South Africa – only to be jilted at the Jan Smuts Airport baggage carousel. Six months grieving and just 21 years old, he was a lost soul with nowhere to go until he was befriended by Kaffir and Mike in a rundown boarding house.

He would often join in the very fierce and competitive inter hotel dart matches played between groups of Aussies and Kiwis. Ted was useless, consistently missing the target, but one night with his team well behind on the scoreboard he threw three remarkable darts to seal a spectacular win.

Thereafter, he was nick named Ted 'The Dart'.

Ted had never set foot on a yacht. He always thought he would fall overboard and resigned himself to do all the menial tasks, such as doing the dishes and cleaning the cabin and toilet.

By now it was September and the month consisted of trips looking at boats of all descriptions and absorbing lots of advice.

"There's a 20 footer at Margate in Kent for a couple of grand," someone offered.

"Too bloody expensive," the others said.

"How about this then – a 30 feet Bermudan cutter moored at Southend-on-Sea?"

"Shit, we've nothing much else to do. Let's take a look," suggested Mike.

The train ride was full of expectation but on inspection the boat was very old and needed a lot of work. Debate on the way home was mixed.

"Yes, we can do it up," Kaffir said.

"It's 200 quid and Christ knows how much we will need to spend on it," Sam countered.

"Yeah okay, let's move on."

Next was a 35 feet Bermudan cutter on racks at Portsmouth. This sounded just right and it was agreed that if the advertisement was true then it would be worth pursuing.

"Listen, we don't want any cock ups with this deal. We'll stop off for a pint and discuss tactics like who's going to say what and who's going to negotiate the price. We need to find as many problems and faults as possible to lower the asking price," said Kaffir.

Time passes quickly when you're excited.

"Sam, it's your Wally Grout."

"We've already had four pints."

"Yeah, but we may as well finish the round."

The five would be sailors eventually arrived at the shipyard to see an old seafaring character wearing an ancient black tattered cap sitting on a stack of coiled rope adjacent to the boat.

"Are you the fellas that's come about this monstrosity?" he said, turning sideways and pointing.

"It's not that bad at least at first sight," said Mike.

"Well, forget it. The owner waited two hours for you and left very pissed off. Your best bet is to go way up north and get yourselves a 50ft ketch or yacht."

The team returned to the pub to ponder this advice and review their financial situation which was dwindling fast. To keep the kitty topped up, Kaffir and Mike joined an agency and was quickly offered carpenters jobs, shop fitting at Oxford Circus for £1.00 an hour. The two smooth-talking Kiwis soon became the foreman's favourite chippies and the rest of the carpenters were gradually dismissed.

Although they were working for an agency and dodging income tax, the company then insisted on employing them as employees at only 65 pence an hour.

"Stuff this, they're ripping us off. I reckon we go back to the agency and have a chat," suggested Mike.

Following some friendly discussions the agency sent them to Nottingham to fit out a jewellery shop in the city centre and generously agreed to provide an additional £2 per day living away allowance. One pound of this was spent on bed and breakfast digs and the other on eight pints of bitter each night. The remaining four pence was always spent on a nourishing bag of salted peanuts to compliment the ale. The pound per hour went into kitty and one decent meal a day.

The pair would return to Highgate each weekend in search of their dream. Also it was to help consume a regular order of 144 dozen cans of Fosters lager bought from the Australian

Forwarding Agency which imported the liquid gold for expatriates.

During this time the stack of magazines grew as Mike continued to check out buying opportunities. Then one day late in October, there it was – a heap of old rubbish lying in a mud berth in Southampton. Mike went down to inspect it. Excitedly he got on the phone.

"I've found it. It's solid. It's what we want. Come on down now!"

It was Sunday 22 October 1972. Everyone met up at midday in the local pub and arrived at the boat yard an hour before it closed. It was low tide and as the advert said, it was sitting in the mud. They crowded around inspecting the hull and keel. A Bermudan yawl, 48ft long with a 9½ft beam. It had no motor or sails. The main hull was constructed with alternating oak and angle iron ribs with mahogany planks fastened with copper rivets. These planks, as with the decks, were corked with cotton and pitch.

The main mast and boom made of spruce in two halves hollowed out and laminated back together, lay on the deck. The mast was made with a curved luff which meant it bent like a banana into the wind. To fit the straight luff main sail, the mast was later winched straight to suit the sails they had purchased. This contributed to the problems they would encounter in the many storms that lay ahead.

Also strewn around the deck was the rigging in a rusted tangled mess with most of the fittings and turnbuckles missing.

A fading copper nameplate was riveted to the bow. It simply said *Babette*.

As far as could be ascertained, *Babette* was built in Sweden for racing in the 1920's. But she had characteristics that made her unsuitable for cruising. The long overhanging counter stern that waves would slap against caused loud annoying drumming noises while at anchor. Her low freeboard and narrow beam made her something more akin to a submarine than a yacht in anything more than a 25-knot breeze. The long boom with its external roller reefing and running back stays, had to be alternately released and tightened on each tacking manoeuvre. It caused havoc on the out-of-control gybes often tearing the sails to shreds when running in big seas.

"Yep, she's in solid and perfect condition. What do the rest of you think?" asked Kaffir. They all looked at each other.

"I'm pissed off spending every weekend looking at broken-down heaps of shit all over England," said Mike.

"We won't find another like her." The others agreed and soon an intermediary for the owner was found.

"No problem. I can do you a deal for £1500."

"Shit, that's a lot."

"Listen, the owner of this yacht is doing time in Wormwood Scrubs prison just outside London."

"You're joking."

"No. He ran out of dough doing it up so he attempted to pull off an armed payroll job. He got violent, got caught and now he's doing a seven year stretch. He needs the money."

Our heroes huddled together, "Look, he needs the dough and we need the boat. Let's offer him £1250."

"Done," agreed the intermediary. "Strictly cash." Everyone shook hands.

Out of earshot Kenny casually asked, "How the hell are we going to pay for it? Kaffir and I are stony broke."

Sam, who had a steady job as a draftsman was fortunately cashed up and came to the party. Ted and Mike scraped together the rest of the investment and in late October the ownership papers changed hands.

During this process, they became friendly with the boat yard owner who plied them with plenty of advice.

"I've got the perfect sail for her, a 40 feet Egyptian cotton sail from an ex-America's Cup boat. It just needs a little cutting down," he offered.

"Yeah okay," said Kaffir.

"I can sell you a radio telephone for £60 and a motor for £200."

"No thanks, mate. We've just run out of money," Kaffir replied.

The challenge now was to get *Babette* from Southampton to a secure berth on the River Thames in London. A number of options were explored. They ranged from installing an inboard diesel motor, rigging the boat and sailing it up The Thames. Another was hiring and securing a big outboard motor on the stern. All were ridiculous and unworkable.

"I reckon we do what we can here and then reassess the situation later," Mike suggested. It was agreed.

Kaffir and Mike started to collect suitable building materials from their worksite and the company's delivery truck driver was bribed to transport it to their Highgate residence. There were many trips to Southampton to measure masts and booms for the eventual fitting of the 40 feet sail.

It was November and London was cold, wet – a place where you went to work in the dark and came home in the dark. It was also the period when Greater London was subject to IRA bomb scares. You might say a bloody miserable place.

The Original five, London 1973. L to R: Ted 'The Dart',
Kenny Nice Guy, Sam, and Kaffer. Front Mike.

Travelling back and forth from Southampton in the pouring rain was hair-raising in the cheap clapped out VW station wagon especially purchased to transport the materials, tools and equipment.

One day the VW lurched sideways, its poor brakes and bald tyres unable to withstand Kaffir's aggressive driving in the rain. In the car's path was an old lady who was quite within her rights walking on the pedestrian crossing. The VW was out of control. Everyone held their breath as the car slid towards her with Kaffir frantically hauling on the steering wheel. A passer-by yelled abuse as he pulled her to safety, the VW missing her by a matter of feet. It was narrow miss and to calm the nerves, it was back to their local pub, 'The Woodman.'

The old VW was then abandoned in a back street.

The Woodman on Archway Road, Highgate, was conveniently located within easy walking distance from home and 250 yards up a hill from Highgate Tube station. It featured two pool tables and flying insects that attacked them in the small beer garden. The locals were good fun and the landlord was extremely happy with the increased patronage the boys provided.

The following weeks were wet and with unreliable transport there were few opportunities to go down to the boat which remained buried in the mud. Instead, Mike and Sam joined Hampstead Rugby Union Club which had club rooms in an old, disused church off Albany Street in Regents Park, Central London.

The club was founded from the ashes of the Centymca (Central YMCA) Rugby Football Club after its members were banished for singing bawdy rugby songs after matches. Instead at Hampstead, the wily Chairman set about producing bawdy song books and three best-selling LP's under the nom-de-plume of the Jock Strap Ensemble. One endearing memory was pop star Millie, who had recorded the hit song, 'My Boy Lollipop' joining in the chorus at one of the early recording sessions.

Once at a Sunday morning recording session and after the choir had warmed up by drinking a barrel of beer, someone vomited over the studio's electrical system. This early morning 'smile at the carpet' caused sparks to fly everywhere. A fire took hold. It was chaos. Everyone did a runner and needless to say, the session was hastily abandoned. The recording contract was torn up!

On another occasion, the Ensemble was invited to sing at a bowling club about an hour from London. The choir met at the clubrooms well before hand downing four or five pints each and then bundled onto the bus with plenty of back-up travellers.

When they arrived, the bowling club had generously lined the bar with two pints of lager per man. Needless to say, this top-up put most over the brink and when the choir lined up in rows, balancing on narrow long gymnasium style raised platforms, disaster struck. The back row overbalanced and as one, they careered backwards, smashing through the century old spacious etched window that overlooked the bowling greens.

The gig was hastily abandoned.

A year or so later, it was alleged that because the secretariat could not account for the song book or LP profits or explain new found wealth, the group decided to disband.

Adjacent to the Hampstead club rooms was a tennis court where, with the help of a dim light mounted on the fence and the use of car headlights, training took place.

Downstairs in the clubhouse were three showers mounted on a rotted, wooden floor. Mike and Sam quickly worked out that it was best to leave training first, in order to get a warm shower before cold water kicked in.

It was a home-from-home where dishwashing liquid was a cheap substitute for shampoo. Upstairs was a great bar and almost without exception, members were there only for the drinking and singing, particularly on match days.

The club was full of characters and the end of season rugby tours to Paris and Switzerland were always highlighted with restaurant runners, overnight slumber in the local jail and hasty exits from whorehouses. The rugby club was also a place with plenty of contacts and one night after training, one of the members discussed the proposed sailing trip with Sam and Mike.

"I know the manager of the Blackfriars roll on, roll off container shipping terminal. If you like, I can ask him to arrange for your yacht to be launched into The Thames at Greenwich."

"Shit, that's fantastic," said Sam.

"Yeah, it'll only cost you a crate of Pimkin beer cans," was the response.

A few days later after a lot of telephone calls and negotiation, a low loader was arranged to transport the boat to the overseas terminal at North Greenwich near to what is now the well-known London landmark known as the Millennium Dome.

"Are you sure North Greenwich is the best place?" Sam asked.

"It's the closest I can get you to London. The boat is too high to transport through the Blackwall Tunnel, a shorter route. You will be able to sail the boat upstream from Greenwich to a secure mooring somewhere else," they were told.

It was at this stage that 'Ted Holmes' joined the team. A product of Takapuna Grammar School on the North Shore in Auckland NZ, he was a huge bloke who spent most of his working life as a scaffolding rigger. Ted had first made contact with Kaffir, Ted and Mike in a bar in South Africa and had heard about the boat on the grapevine. Big and confrontational when drunk, his mop of blond afro hair was matched by an unkempt beard and a big appetite.

He was often arrested when ashore and would steal food whenever the opportunity arose. He liked to have a smoke too. He was the sort of guy that knew everything, was going to do lots of things, but actually did fuck all! But it was always reassuring to have him around when out on 'the town'.

He was commonly known as Kiwi Ted. No one actually knew his surname.

It was Friday, 2 March 1973 and there was great excitement in the air. Mike, the two Teds and Kaffir travelled to Southampton by train early that morning to the boat yard. The day had been chosen because the massive spring tide would allow the boat to lift out of the mud making it easier to hoist out and load onto the transporter.

The hull being loaded onto the transporter

It was 10am, high tide and everything proceeded like clockwork.

"What a magnificent sight!" Ted 'the Dart' exclaimed as the hull hung in the air before being placed on the tray of the transporter.

With the boat secure and ready for its next journey there were lots of photos taken. There was a soothing sense of satisfaction welling within all those who watched.

It was a long trip back to London using alternative routes to avoid low overhead bridges and restricted roads. At 7.30pm, *Babette* arrived at North Greenwich Overseas Ferry Terminal, just below the Blackwall Tunnel. The transporter was whisked through to the edge of Phoenix Wharf where a big crane was waiting to drop *Babette* into the river.

"Don't worry boys, I'll tie her up," said Kiwi Ted. Trusting in Kiwi Ted's expertise would soon prove to be an expensive mistake.

With the yacht's hull moored, it was back to The Woodman and 'Chez Highgate' where, with Sam, celebratory drinks went well into the early hours of Saturday morning.

At 7.00am, there was a knock on the door. It was an English Bobby.

"Does a Mike Anderson live here?"

The usual procedure in those days was, 'no Mike Anderson here. He left for South Africa a few days ago'.

The policeman said, "Would you mind telling him when he comes back that his boat has just sunk!" Hearing this, Mike immediately leapt out of bed and ran to the door.

"No, No. The plane was delayed, I didn't go. What's the problem?"

"Well, you have quite a few problems," retorted the policeman. "I think that you'd better get down to the Thames as quickly as you can. It's chaos down there."

"Shit!"

Kiwi Ted had tied a line from the bow and another from the stern, both going up to a bollard situated amidships and 20 feet above the yacht. As soon as the tide came in and with no yield, the yacht simply went up and down in the 8-knot tide. It swivelled on its mooring lines, wedged under the wharf and sank. As the boat sunk, the line to the stern pulled the cleat out of the deck and it was only the more secure bow line that stopped the boat from disappearing downstream.

The fact was our sailors didn't know The Thames had a tide and at that point it rose to 18feet. *Babette* was hanging by one line vertically in the water with her nose just poking out of the swirling River Thames.

The trip to the river was in relative silence. At the wharf gates the manager, a ruddy faced rotund individual was waiting with his arms folded.

"Come up to my office. We need to have a serious chat," he said.

The sailors sat passively in front of an old wooden desk that was littered with maps and a chipped coffee cup with a dark stain rimming the inside. The manager with his arms still folded, laid out the facts.

"You've got 12 hours to get the sunken hull out of the water. There's a ship due to moor at the Overseas Terminal within 48 hours. That wreck of yours is a danger to all on the water. If the boat isn't removed quickly, the police will come in with a salvage crew, pick it up, put it on a barge and that will be that," he said. Our would-be heroes looked on in stony silence. The manager lent forward.

"Listen, the boss is a pretty reasonable sort of person. He's the governor of the whole ferry terminal. I've had a chat with him and he said he would look after you. So get your arses over to his office. Go on. Get cracking!"

And cracking they did. Soon they were knocking on the door of a small office, overlooking the wharf.

"You blokes are all Kiwis and Aussies, right? I'll always remember the hospitality, I had in New Zealand. It was bloody fantastic in your country so I'm happy to pay a little back," were his opening remarks, "everything here including the cranes is at your disposal."

"We really appreciate that," said a very subdued Kiwi Ted. "What should we do now?"

"Get some divers to inspect the condition of the hull," replied the governor. The crew trooped silently out of the office.

"Where the fuck do we find a couple of divers at such short notice?" Kiwi Ted asked.

"That's your problem, Ted. Get over to that phone box and start going through the Yellow Pages," Kaffir ordered.

After a number of calls that went nowhere, a team of two divers were eventually found and arrived on the wharf just before dusk on Saturday night. They were welcomed immediately with some ice cold Fosters larger – the stable diet of Aussies and Kiwis overseas. After the 'get-to-know you' session was over, the divers attached another line to secure the boat and then put some sleeves around *Babette*.

"That'll do. We'll see you at 8.00am for an inspection to figure how to get this thing out and onto a container," one said.

The night passed without incident.

It was Sunday morning, 4 March 1973.

There was plenty of action on the wharf. The authorities had wasted no time in making their presence felt. The Blackwall Fire Brigade had been summoned and The Port of London police was in attendance.

"We just want to keep an eye on things," the police spokesperson said.

The divers reported there was no damage to the hull and it could be safely lifted out. The wharf crane was lowered, fixed to the bow and *Babette* was hoisted gently over a shipping container trolley. Suddenly, the yacht's rotten transom partially broke away as *Babette* was placed on an angle to the container. She was still in one piece much to everyone's relief. While *Babette* was in the air the fire brigade pumped out the water.

"But what about the mud and silt?" Kiwi Ted nervously asked.

"Silly question, Ted. Cleaning out the boat will be your job," Sam said.

"No, no, that's all right, we'll deal with it," the fire chief said sensing trouble in the camp.

The fire crew went into action again. It was a combination of tilt, pump water into the hull then pump the mud out of the back. Two hours later, *Babette* was nestling in a cradle hanging from the crane its struts exposed.

The crane then delicately released the boat back into The Thames. Everyone was happy including the river police, who were impressed with the whole operation. The crew went into a huddle.

"What do we do now?" Kaffir worriedly asked. "After we've paid the divers, we won't have any money left for all the other work and it is impossible to do a runner from these blokes."

The other police looked on.

"These lads are in all sorts of trouble and frankly I don't want them on my patch. I just don't like the look of them," one said.

"Why don't we send them up stream and let another jurisdiction worry about them?"

The other police nodded with approval.

"I know of a mooring three miles upstream at Kew, in Richmond. It's yours and we'll tow the boat there for nothing."

"That's bloody fantastic! Thanks," Mike said gratefully.

To settle *Babette* into her new home it took two different police tows. The first was quickly attached.

Sitting on the hull in the early afternoon they had a grandstand view of the City of London. They were towed under 15 famous bridges and passed many of London's historic buildings. The three-mile journey upstream started just south of the Blackwall Tunnel. It passed the Cutty Sark, an old 19th century tea and wool sailing clipper which stood in dry dock, near the Greenwich Pier. But in June 2007, it was burnt to the ground leaving an estimated £30m worth of damage. Moored beside it was gipsy Moth 1V, the yacht in which Francis Chichester who was later knighted made his sole circumnavigation of the world in 1966.

Those on board were in wonder of what was unfolding before their eyes.

"It's the best view of London anyone can have!" exclaimed Mike.

"Yeah, but there seem to be a hell of a lot of bridges. I hope we can avoid them when we set sail for Australia," replied Sam.

Soon it was late afternoon and the bridge at Westminster came into view. Another police launch was waiting to take over the tow for the final leg and little was said by either party. With no money, it was best to do nothing, say nothing and know nothing. The police tow made fast progress along the smooth calm Thames, passing jetties, wharfs and boat houses at every nook and cranny of the river.

The boys were in awe of hope and adventure. The lights in the city buildings were gradually being switched on. The numerous reflections on the swirling black river was soothing to their dampened spirits.

The boat finally arrived at its new home at Strand-on-the Green in Chiswick, Kew. The police tow manoeuvred *Babette* to her new mooring in the middle of the river next to Oliver's Island, just a short walk downstream from Kew Bridge. It was directly opposite and just an easy row from *Babette* to The City Barge pub, which was to become their new home-away-from-home.

The City Barge was the local to a rather posh and exclusive enclave where former fishermen's cottages now sell for more than £1 million each.

It was built in 1484 and originally called 'The Navigator's Arms'. It was renamed in the 1880s when the State Barge of the Lord Mayor of London was moored on The Thames in almost the same spot *Babette* inherited.

The pub had two drinking areas. The boys made the 'lower old bar' their own. It had a low exposed beam ceiling, a couple of fire places, wooden chairs, a red tiled floor, and numerous old-fashioned brass and gas light fittings. It also had a darts board.

The City Barge was where almost all the decisions relating to the yacht were made – some good, but mostly bad.

Despite the pub being almost 40 miles inland, the river Thames still had an ugly tidal rise and fall of around 23 feet. At certain times of the month when the moon was either new or full, the river would cover the riverside walkway and if it was not for a steel door it would flood the old bar. During the spring and summer equinoxes when the tides were exceptionally high, the river would completely cover the tables outside on the footpath and lap inches below the pub's windows. There was nothing better than being held captive inside a pub!

The Port of London Authority branch was comfortable with this mooring too as one of their offices was just 400 yards downstream. They were to try with mixed results, to keep a sharp eye on the antics of the crew.

As the police tow left, the river captain lent over the side.

"This mooring is yours and if you aren't working on this boat every day from now then you'll lose it and your sailing days will be over."

The next challenge was to clean the mud and silt out of the bilges following the disaster at North Greenwich. The sailors were smart. Mates came down from near and far to help.

The smell of acids and chemicals from the thick red muck was overwhelming. Cleaning it up took such a long and tedious time that the health of everyone was in danger.

The Port of London Police branch could see the operation was struggling, so they kindly donated a dinghy. It was a solid, heavy and clinker-built two-man dinghy which had been tied up below their office and had not been used for a year or two.

The cleaning was thirsty work and these were thirsty young men. There were regular three hour drinking sessions on an early Sunday afternoon.

Returning in the dinghy, getting covered in mud, then rowing back to The City Barge for the evening session began to take its toll. Lack of food and hangovers became a regular pastime.

Working on the boat, Chiswick, Kew

It took the next two months to clean the boat inside and out. Meanwhile The Port of London Authority, true to their word, came by every day to keep an eye on the activity.

The long meetings in the pub resulted in some decisions being made. First priority was to repair the rot in the transom and the aft deck. The whole aft deck was pulled off and recovered.

The cabin was reconstructed and fibre glassed. But the rigging remained a mess. Strewn all over the deck and hanging in the water it really needed replacing, but with little money it became a legacy of the refit.

"What are you doing Kaffir?" Ted 'The Dart' asked one day.

"I've mixed up a big brew of fibreglass to pour down all the holes on the deck."

"I'll give you a hand," volunteered Ted.

Together they filled most of the holes with fibreglass. Suddenly without warning, the surrounding deck timbers burst into flames.

"Shit!" Kaffir yelled. "I've put too much hardener in the mixture. It's over reacted. Get the fire extinguisher."

"Kaffir, we don't have one!"

"Then get a bucket brigade going, you fucking idiot."

Leaning over the side a bucket was passed between the two and water was splashed over the deck. A gathering crowd outside the pub looked on. Soon an arid smell and swirling black smoke filled the air.

"Wow, what a relief! I don't think there's any damage," a relieved Kaffir exclaimed.

"You know what?" said Ted. "I reckon the scorching colour adds to the overall character of the boat."

The next few months were spent around the South of England scrounging equipment and materials and visiting and revisiting chandler shops. Their methods of transport changed by the month, as various cheap old cars broke down and were abandoned all over London.

"I've been having a bit of yarn with a guy in the pub," Kenny said one day. "He told me every type of pleasure craft using Britain's waterways must be registered and licensed. Unless the navigation certificate and registration number is displayed at all times we will cop a fine."

"Yeah, I've been thinking about that too," said Kaffir. "If we get the paperwork done now it will avoid unnecessary harassment by the water cops and the various custom authorities."

It was agreed to take the bill of sale and register *Babette* at the registration office in Reading. But on arrival, a surprise awaited them.

"Sorry, but you don't have a company seal on this sale note. Your bill of sale is worthless. We can't help you here," they were told.

"You must be joking," said Mike. "We paid a lot of money for this luxury yacht."

"Then you must go back to the place where you bought it and get them to execute the sale properly," was the reply.

"Shit, this is a bit of a worry," Kaffir said as they left the building. "But we've got no choice."

So, it was back to the Southampton shipyard where *Babette* was first discovered. The so-called friendly manager who had sold them the yacht gave them 'the cold shoulder'.

"I don't know what you're talking about. I don't know any *Babette*."

"That's bullshit," said an angry Kiwi Ted. "It's your fucking signature on this bill of sale."

'"Yeah, but I don't know anything about that boat."

"Listen mate, we're going to sue you and report you to the coppers for a false sale. Give us our fucking money back or I'll hang you out of the window," snarled Kiwi Ted.

"Let me check out some paperwork," the manager said, his two hands raised defensively in the air and obviously stalling for time.

"We'll be back in an hour. Have some answers or you'll be in the morgue," Kiwi Ted yelled slamming the door behind him.

The crew adjourned to the pub furious as to what was unfolding. "I'm going to hammer the shit out of him," Kiwi Ted said, sculling his third pint.

"Let's be cool about it, Ted," Mike said calmly as they began to make their way back to the office precisely one hour later.

"Well, what's the story?" Kiwi Ted challenged.

"Okay, okay, okay," said the manager nervously. "To be quite honest, it wasn't our boat to sell. The guy that owns it is in the slammer and he owed us a lot of money in mooring and maintenance fees. While he's in jail, the boat is just sitting here accruing fees and charges. The only way to recoup our money was to sell it. We got our £1200 thanks to you guys but we never got around to claim the registration papers from the owner."

"Shit, you wouldn't believe it. We've got a boat that will always be unregistered. Fuck me," said Ted shaking his head.

So *Babette* was never officially registered. The only places that picked it up were the two English speaking ports – Gibraltar and Malta. Customs queried it, but the sailors always spun the bullshit and both ports decided to put it in the 'too hard basket', overlooking two of the most important rules of the high seas. 'Who are you and under what flag are you flying!'

Life on the river was full of incidents and foolhardy exploits. Just upstream from their mooring was an ex-trawler fishing boat owned by the local Richmond troop of Sea Scouts. It was very solid; double ended with high gunwales and stood about 10 feet out of the water.

As you would expect, the scouts kept it nicely painted with shiny polished woodwork and clean, smooth sails. Occasionally they would do day trips up or down the river and return in the afternoon. Depending on which way the tide was running, with great expertise they would gently manoeuvre from behind or above *Babette* and re-attach to their buoy.

It was the Easter break when the Sea Scouts informed the *Babette* crew that they would be cruising to Holland and would be back after the long weekend. On their return, they were spotted coming up river with their powerful diesel engine pushing a hefty bow against a very fast out-going current.

All the Sea Scouts impeccably dressed in their uniforms, stood to attention around the safety rail waiting for orders to moor. They gently passed *Babette* and on approaching their buoy the order was barked out, 'hook the mooring buoy!'

The engine was cut but unfortunately they didn't hook up. Before they could restart the motor, the boat swung sideways in the current and was drifting straight for *Babette*. Kaffir and the boys looked up in horror.

"Shit, we're going to get rammed," Sam yelled.

"Don't panic. Just sit tight. There's nothing we can do except sue them for a new yacht," Kaffir said.

The scouts looked down with that 'Sorry guys, but we think it's going to hurt you more than us' look in their faces. The trawler continued towards them. *Babette's* crew braced themselves for the impending collision.

"Hold on and be ready to jump overboard," said a panic stricken Sam. The trawler was on them within seconds and the impact was like a bolt of thunder. Then to their astonishment, on contact, *Babette's* very slender bow jagged an enormous hole through the trawler's planking causing a loud cracking and groaning sound.

"Fuck me. You're a hero, baby," said 'The Dart' dancing around on deck.

"There's no damage here, only your pride," yelled Kaffir to the panicking Sea Scouts as they glided by.

Later in The City Barge, the day's events were recounted time and time again and incidents like that and others were to give the crew great confidence for the journey ahead.

Adjacent to *Babette's* mooring was an old launch called, '*The Nan*'. It had been there for months and was full of provisions and a wide selection of tools. One day Mike suggested to Kaffir, "Why don't we go aboard and check it out?"

"Great idea," Kaffir replied. "I reckon it's been abandoned."

Clambering aboard, they immediately helped themselves to a tin of 'heat up pie'.

"This tucker's not bad," said Mike heating himself another pie.

Mike on Babette moored next to The Nan

Over the next few days their confidence grew. They ate all the food and in the following months they cleaned the whole boat out of the navigation equipment and tools.

The Nan's deck was shaped like a barge with plenty of space which became a storage area for them. It gradually became littered with rigging, gear, sheets of plywood, discarded planking and tools.

Then one afternoon the inevitable happened – the owner turned up. He was not happy!

"Get those fucking tools and rubbish off my boat," he screamed, not knowing that they were actually his.

He began wielding an axe and the swearing continued.

"If they're not cleared in five minutes, I promise you I will chop all your mooring ropes. I don't want any of your crap on my boat."

"You heard him," Kaffir said. "We'd better do what we're told."

For the next five minutes of so, everything was thrown into the dinghy or bought aboard *Babette* and stored below deck.

The owner did not let up. "If you bastards ever set foot on my launch again you'll feel the impact of this axe."

That night in The City Barge, the crew tried to do a stock take of their booty but eventually gave up as the pints took over their thought processes.

Shortly after the registration debacle, discussion grew about changing the name of the boat.

"We need a name that reflects us better," Mike suggested.

"Isn't it bad luck to change the name of a boat?" Ted 'The Dart' queried.

"Yeah, that's what they say but I agree with Mike. I think we should change her name."

For the next few weeks, many hours were spent in pubs discussing names and writing the best ones onto assorted beer coasters.

"Here's the short list," said Mike shuffling all the beer coasters like a pack of cards. "*Bordello, Dawn Breaker, Beer Chaser, Aqua Holic, Wind Breaker, Nauti, Party Boys, Passing Wind, Full of Seamen, Seas the Day, Pier Pressure, The Codfather, Eggs–ta–sea, SuperDong, Boobie Bouncer, Cirrhosis of the River, The Salty Swallow, Sex Sea, Fish and Chicks, Wet Dreams* and *Blow Job*."

Everyone had a good laugh before Sam spoke up.

"Shit, I dunno how they'll go down with the authorities," he said. "She's such a nice and prized lady. We need a much friendlier name, don't we?"

"What about *Shagwell* then?" piped up Kiwi Ted.

"I've got it," Ted 'The Dart' said enthusiastically. "Why don't we call her *Antipodean*?" We're all Kiwis or Aussies aren't we?"

They all nodded in agreement, "*Antipodean*! Yes, that's more like it."

The rest of the week was spent toasting, 'to the *Antipodean*'.

To bring the new name luck, a South African silver rand donated by Sam, was put under the main mast when it was finally fitted into position a few months later.

Provisioning of *Antipodean* was on going. And their confidence on all things nautical continued to grow. They thought it was their right to go and take whatever they wanted off any other boat. Many a night little sorties were undertaken up and down the river.

On one occasion after a session in the City Barge, Mike decided to assist the project by going off on his own to plunder what he thought was an abandoned launch.

Scrambling aboard, he began rummaging through the cupboards and under the storage seats. But, unbeknown to him an elderly lady lived on board.

"Hey, what do you think you're doing? Who are you?"

Mike froze.

"Nothing, I think I'm lost."

"Get off my boat, you useless brat," she said throwing an empty gin bottle in his direction.

Mike obliged and rowed away.

"You should have followed procedure and consulted the acquisitions committee. You could have been killed out there," said Kaffir.

Downstream there was a big expensive looking launch equipped with flags, charts and other equipment that *Antipodean* needed.

"If we can get most of that stuff we'll be right," Kaffir told Sam and Ted the Dart.

"Here's a plan. You guys drop me off at the launch and then pick me up, say in an hour. There are some huge willow trees that line the river edge. You guys can hide there from the police patrols and then row out collect me with the booty."

It was agreed.

"I need a drink first," said Sam. The three of them headed for the City Barge and had a long session before being thrown out at stumps. They rowed downstream, the small dinghy weaving from side to side. Kaffir was dropped off at the launch and climbed on board carrying a large sack. He then proceeded to take the beads out of the cabin window gingerly removing the glass and then helped himself to everything he could lay his hands on.

Safely anchored in the lee of the towering willows Sam and 'The Dart' waited, trying to keep warm in the cold night air. The police patrol passed every 30 minutes. Up and down, to and fro it went. Meanwhile, Kaffir patiently waited for the pickup, hiding in the shadows of the cabin.

"Where the fuck are they?" he cursed under his breath.

Too many pints of lager had taken effect. Sam and 'The Dart' had fallen asleep! Looking upstream, Kaffir saw a series of buoys, all linked together with big thick chains. Murmuring to himself, he figured it was feasible to manoeuvre along this combination back to *Antipodean* without the dinghy. Slipping over board he grappled with the swinging chains and only just made it to the first buoy. At that moment, a patrol came into view. Ducking his head to avoid being seen, he over balanced and fell straight into the Thames. The sack, full with flags, maps and a lot of other gear slowly began to sink.

"Is anyone there?" someone on the police launch boomed through a loud hailer about 50 feet away.

"Shit!"

Kaffir was busily treading water, his head barely above the surface as he circled the buoy hiding from the police. He could hear them trying to retrieve the sack out of the Thames.

"Pass the boat hook. I can hardly reach what looks to be a body floating below me."

The police hauled the sack aboard. "This is all a bit strange. Something's a bit dodgy here," he heard one of them say to the other.

"Yeah, it looks like this stuff has been stolen off someone's boat," the other replied.

The police continued to circle peering over the side flashing a search light up and down the river. Kaffir continued to duck dive around the buoy before the patrol eventually headed off. Exhausted, he swam back to *Antipodean* and crawled into his bunk.

At 5.00am, Sam and 'The Dart' returned tired, stiff and very hung-over.

The next morning the police patrol boat pulled alongside.

"Boys, there's been a lot of stealing going on. Make sure you lock your boat up."

Kiwi Ted who now had accumulated a record of empty promises on just about everything was copping a fair bit of flak from the others, so he attempted to get back in their good books.

"I've just purchased a real bargain for the boat," he told them in the pub late one afternoon.

"Yeah, what's that?"

"It's an eight feet polystyrene dinghy. It cost only £7.00. I'll row it back to the boat and you can judge for yourselves."

Ted's huge frame towered above the small dinghy as he began to clumsily row out from the shore. After 50 yards the dinghy suddenly wobbled from side to side, floundered, slowly turned over and under Ted's weight, broke in half. Ted was in the drink, screaming profanities as his acquisition floated downstream. Everyone roared with laughter.

"I'll kill the bastard that sold me this," screamed Kiwi Ted, hauling himself back onto the riverbank.

"No, you won't, Ted," said Kaffir. "That bargain was not going anywhere. It should have been finished off in fibreglass. There's probably dozens of these things at the bottom of the Thames bought by wankers like you!"

Antipodean's mooring at Kew

Oliver's Island was located in the middle of the Thames, slightly upstream from the City Barge. It was a fascinating place, heavily wooded with cascading weeping willows around most of its shoreline and was a haven for several species of birds, including herons and cormorants.

The rest of the island was littered with junk. Old hand operated machinery and huge stacks of old wooden beams lay amongst the long grass. It got its name from a story that Oliver Cromwell used it as a hiding place during the English Civil War and that there was a tunnel from The Bell and Crown public house to the island. This was a myth of course. Locals in the Barge explained that it was the site of the last boat builders' yard on the Thames within the boundaries of London.

There was also an old crane on the island. It was rusty and barely workable but would serve its purpose in the weeks ahead. The island was also used by The Port of London Authority Police to dispose of old boats that had been abandoned on the river. They would tow the boats close to shore, tie them to a tree on the island and at one of the convenient low tides douse them with petrol and torch them. It was always a drawn out process because the police would first pick over and keep anything that they might find of value. Then they would sail by the *Antipodean* and tell the crew to 'help yourselves to any bits and pieces that you can salvage'.

Usually there was only about two hours to scavenge for parts or to unscrew or unbolt anything that might be useful. 'The burnings' would always be watched with great interest. It was amazing just how quickly wooden boats can disappear to the water line.

One afternoon after a few months working on the boat, someone yelled out from the river bank.

"Hey, how's it going?"

It was Kenny Nice Guy. Sam rowed over and brought him back to the boat.

"I've been working in Canada and heard about you guys in the Earls Court pub. I thought I would come down and check out the boat."

"Yeah, it's a bit of a slog now," Sam explained. "We've been to all points of England trying to find a motor. The guys at the rugby club and in the pub have given plenty of advice, but no engine!"

"Kenny, there's an old London taxi cab motor for sale in the Exchange and Mart. It's been marinised, has a heat exchanger and a crash gear box with three gears. What do you think?" Mike asked.

"Three gears make it useless really. You only need one forward gear and reverse. In reality though, a diesel taxi cab motor is a pretty reliable engine. Check it out and it it's any good, buy it."

It was duly inspected but with some apprehension. It was snapped up for the pricey sum of £150. Kenny assured everyone he was the perfect person to install the engine. The team held a brief meeting and unanimously agreed to give him a 'free crewing job' on the boat for his services. After all, the assembled crew knew nothing about sailing and even less about installing a taxi motor intended to help get them across the Pacific.

Kenny was the man of the moment. He installed the motor and after much difficulty it was bolted to the hull. Next, using some sort of mitre tool, he aligned the prop shaft with the drive.

Perfect!

A week or so later, Kaffir began fiddling with what he thought was a problem with the shaft.

"While I sort this out, it might be a good idea to paint a water line around the boat Sam."

"Yeah, okay."

Kaffir set about removing the bracket which secured the shaft to the hull, but his lack of expertise left four gaping holes just above the river. As dusk descended, they decided to adjourn to The City Barge for drinks and then spend the night aboard and finish their work in the morning.

At closing time, they rowed back but by then the tide had come in.

"Sam, you fuckin' idiot, you've painted the water line about a metre too low! No one can see it. It's fuckin' useless."

He continued to lay the verbal on Sam who was pretty sheepish and continued to cop an earful as they clambered on-board and down to their bunks.

"Hey, what's this? There's water pissing through the hull. The joints flooded. We're really in the shit. Bloody hell, Kaffir – who's the fuckin' idiot now?"

The floor was awash with silt, mud, and oily water.

"You're useless! Why didn't you leave all that stuff to Kenny?"

"Yeah, yeah, okay, okay, we're equal now," Kaffir said, embarrassed.

It was panic stations. Sam went ashore and rang Highgate and in the early morning the others assembled to help with the bailing. The commotion also brought the police, who as usual looked on.

"Can you help us?" pleaded The Dart. Familiar with their activities, the police did.

"Here, use this," they responded throwing them a bucket.

"Bloody typical pigs," murmured Kiwi Ted.

The motor was not looking good. The electrics and shaft were buried in everything the Thames could offer. It was back to square one again. It took three weeks to bail and clean below decks, replace the bolts and get ship shape again.

Through all this Kenny worked tirelessly on the motor, before eventually declaring that it was time to test it with a sea trial. The motor was started and as everyone held their collective breath. *Antipodean* motored up and down the river without a problem.

Everyone cheered with delight.

At about this time, Sam began working with Alexander Gibbs and Partners, a large inner city engineering and drafting company. It was off Victoria Street in St James and about a quarter of a mile from St James Park Tube station.

The building was right next to Scotland Yard. When you looked out the window on the sixth floor, you could see the rotating 'Scotland Yard' sign, made famous in many UK police dramas. Directly opposite in another building was a large typing pool crowded with lovely English secretaries.

Sam had been a draftsman in Australia, completing his trade shortly after leaving school and easily secured a job when the company won a big contract to monitor traffic flows all over London. He quickly discovered that the work was basic and anybody, irrespective of intelligence, could trace traffic flow grids on a large angled drafting board. Draftsmen were in short supply and they needed more.

The Chairman of the company was a fanatical skier who had skied at Coronet Peak and The Remarkables in the South Island, New Zealand. In the pub, an idea quickly grew on how to get a job there. All you had to do was get the head of the company to talk about skiing.

Your author had just returned from Europe and was stony broke.

"Come and work with us," Sam suggested.

"Shit Sam, I know nothing about drafting," I replied. But these were desperate times and I was desperate. So I called and arranged an interview.

When I arrived, I was shown into a very large office. The oak panelled walls were lined with oil paintings of the company's chairmen down through the years. There was a large ceiling fan quietly whirling away above an enormous walnut desk which dominated the room. It was completely bare except for a green blotter and to the left was a photograph of the chairman's family. Behind the desk in an oversized leather chair sat a small man with horn rimmed glasses. I was nervous!

After a bit of a chit-chat, he asked, "What's your drafting experience?"

"Well, I was trained in Dunedin with the local council and spent a lot of time working with the traffic department." Before he could respond and as instructed by Sam, continued. "Before coming overseas, I spent a lot of time in Queenstown with the local council examining ways to improve access roads to Coronet Peak, The Remarkables and the Cardrona ski fields."

"Wow!" he exclaimed. "You're a skier!"

"Yes, I am," when in fact, I had never touched a ski in my life. The next 20 or so minutes were dominated by him waxing lyrically about New Zealand; the skis that he owned and his dream of returning. I nodded and agreed on all points. Then there was a pregnant silence. Then he simply said, "Ohhhh, okay, when can you start?"

"Tomorrow," I replied.

The next morning I was met by the project manager, an Englishman called Richard. He greeted me warmly but when he discovered that I was a New Zealander, he went a bit cold, "I suppose you worked for Dunedin Council too."

"Indeed," I responded.

In the room there were about 30 drawing boards manned by assorted Kiwis and Aussies but only two qualified draftsmen who circulated helping the others.

It was also the period in London when the IRA was active and bomb scares were frequent. Being next to Scotland Yard made our building an obvious target and it was constantly being evacuated. Strange, but the bomb scares always seemed to occur when there was a cricket test match or some other important sporting event taking place involving Australia or New Zealand.

Conveniently, when this happened everyone always made a hasty retreat to the local, called 'The Two Chairmen' in Dartmouth St, about half a mile from the office. Inside it was dark, dingy and pokey. It was lined with old fashioned wall paper, had dark panelling, a black and grey patterned papered ceiling, pew seating and a cracked tiled fireplace. Behind the bar were three fading murals depicting 18th century scenes, coated with grime. But it did have a dart board, a decent TV and few customers. Many hours were spent there on full pay.

There was very little work done when everyone returned to the drafting boards. To amuse ourselves we would 'throw kisses' towards the typing pool opposite. It was great fun to look at their surprised faces as they lined the window to watch us.

After a couple of months and with winter looming, it was time to move on. At the farewell drinks in the Two Chairmen, I approached Richard and thanked him for the opportunity to work with the company.

"When I come back from Europe will you employ me again, please?"

"Stan," he said. "Don't count on it!"

Busy at work before stepping the mast

It was now time to install the main mast which had been lying on the deck since the boat was purchased. It was all hands on deck as *Antipodean* was moved to a position 25 yards off Oliver's Island. The old rusted crane swung out over a narrow walkway and hung over the boat. The mast was slung around the crane's boom and then swaying to and fro, manoeuvred above the deck. The mast was slowly lowered into position and prior to being inserted the South African silver rand was placed at its base.

The mast is stepped but more work to be done

The crew gathered on deck, drinks in hand for a toast.

"Good luck and God speed," was repeated over and over again. There was a glowing sense of pride amongst them as the raised pint glasses clinked against each other.

The objective had been to set sail in June 1973, 10 months after the yacht was purchased. But it was now July and there was an increased urgency to get the boat totally prepared for the voyage ahead. A final sea trial was planned to see how *Antipodean* would motor with the mast in place. The crew were nervous of the outcome because with the mast inserted, it put more weight onto the forward half of the yacht. No one knew what to expect.

The nominated day arrived. Six crew, plus about 10 hangers on, crammed onto *Antipodean*. The motor kicked in for about 100 yards and then cut out, right in front of the pub. At this particular time the tide was running out. *Antipodean* began to drift out of control all over the river, finally heading for Chiswick Rail Bridge, just 250 yards downstream. First it brushed against a tiny wharf near a small boathouse. Then side swiped two unmanned buoys.

"Shit, we've got to stop her. There's no way known the mast will fit underneath the bridge," yelled Sam.

Antipodean carried on downstream heading straight for the bridge. A crowd of on lookers gathered on the river bank to watch the drama unfold. All on board began waving their arms and yelling for help. Then, within 100 feet from disaster, a motor boat zoomed to their rescue.

"Grab this," someone yelled throwing them a rope. Hastily the rope was secured and *Antipodean* began a slow tow back up to its mooring. The large crowd on the walkway and the drinkers from the City Barge taunted and laughed at the crew's misfortune.

"Damn, this is very embarrassing. I'm sorry guys," said Kenny. "I'll work on the motor over the next week until it's reliable."

The next project was to convert the huge cotton sail off the early A Class America's Cup boat, purchased from the middleman in Southampton. This involved cutting the top off for the mizzen and then creating and hand-sewing the mainsail.

Over the next few weekends, they would lug the big heavy oversize sail to nearby Highgate Park, spread it out and each person would sit on a corner and sew and sew and sew!

"This is fuckin' useless – a waste of time. It's giving me the shits all this sewing," said Ted the Dart.

"My fingers are stuffed."

"Yeah, I agree. There must be a better way to do this. Let's ask around the rugby club. Maybe someone has a contact that can help," Mike suggested. A rugby club member gladly provided the name of a tent maker who took over the onerous job.

It was also decided to examine the old World War 11 life raft purchased for £17.50. They had been told it was a six to 10 man raft that had been clamped under the wing of an old war transporter plane.

"I'm worried about this," said Mike. "It won't save our lives if we don't know how big it is and what's in it. It could be bigger than our front room."

The raft was placed in the centre of the cramped front room at Highgate and ignited from the gas cylinder. It began to quickly expand. It grew bigger and bigger and bigger.

"Christ, look out, it's going to fill the room and smash the telly," yelled the Dart. "Everyone grab it and get it outside."

It was dragged through a pair of French doors, cracking the frame and out onto the small overgrown back garden. It continued to expand. It was massive. Gradually, it took shape.

It was a double ring life raft with its outer walls four feet high. A zip up conical roof gradually emerged. Stored on board were provisions, neatly packed and labelled. Flares and an emergency manual completed the huge World War 11 rubber duck. There it was, parked in the middle of a back yard in Highgate with nowhere to go and no gas left in the cylinder.

"What do we do now?" asked Sam.

"Crush it back into shape and pray we can find someone to re-gas the cylinder under pressure with CO_2," Kaffir replied.

The task to have this done was unsuccessful. Local gas suppliers exclaimed it was against the law.

"You must be joking. We're not mad. We'll be liable and these things are obsolete anyway," was the general response wherever they went.

So it was decided to keep it in the hope that someone at a Mediterranean port or another country would refill it.

The rubber duck was eventually secured on the deck of *Antipodean*. It wasn't until the following year that the raft was eventually released at sea. It was an irresponsible thing to do to let an empty life raft float around the ocean. But, this was the *Antipodean*!

Some very old parachute emergency flares had also been purchased from the very generous intermediary who could lay his hands on anything at a very, very cheap price.

The boys were really keen to see how they worked. So in the early hours of a Sunday morning after another heavy drinking session at The Woodman, it was time to 'have some fun'.

"Let's fire one up and see how high it goes," Kaffir suggested. The flare was gently positioned and propped in a bucket and then lit. Everyone ran for cover.

Whoosh! The flare lit up the sky over Highgate and its environs. What a spectacle. The sky emblazoned in red. It hung there sparkling like a sky rocket for a minute or two, before fading in the darkness.

"Christ isn't that a beautiful sight? No worries about being rescued at sea if we let one of those go!"

Another thing that had been occupying everyone's mind was exactly how to cross the Pacific safely. It was realised that navigational skills would be necessary.

"Sam, you're good with figures and stuff. We reckon you should be our navigator," said Mike late one afternoon.

"Hell, boys, I don't know a thing about navigation."

"Well, it's time you did."

Sam was enrolled in a three-month night school navigational course, held twice a week including Friday nights. But Sam didn't like to miss out on the long Friday night drinking sessions at the pub, missing all the stories, the yarns, the darts, the hopes, the bull shit. He couldn't bear not to be part of the action. On the third Friday evening of the intensive course, Sam was first into the pub buying pints of 'light and bitter' for everyone.

"Shit Sam, what the fuck are you doing here?" You're meant to be at the navigational school," he was asked.

"It's all bull shit. You turn right at the Thames Estuary and then turn left at Gibraltar and we are in the Med," Sam replied, handing around the pints. "Then I'll refer to the atlas which will show the open sea. No worries!"

"Okay, Sam," they said. "You know what you're doing."

The final trial of the installed taxi motor

It was now August 1973.

After two sinkings, one rescue and two river trials, *Antipodean* was ready for its maiden voyage down the Thames and into the open sea. There was great excitement, apprehension and fear!

Before they headed off, Kaffir said to Sam, "I'm up in the bow just going to use the privacy of your cabin to say goodbye to my sweetheart Margaret."

"No, you're not!"

"Now, now, Sam, you need to have a more generous and Christian attitude about sharing if we're to get along on the voyage ahead."

"Just be out of there by closing time."

There were six sailors, Kaffir, Mike, Sam, the two Teds and Kenny Nice Guy. The problem was that six into five berths do not go so there was always one hot berth.

An old guy from The Port of London Authority who had befriended them, rowed out and yelled, "Before you go, come and see me."

So they did. He lifted up a hatch on the pontoon and stored below was an anti-fouling chain, ropes, a heavy fisherman's anchor and assorted provisions.

"I've been collecting and then keeping all this stuff for you. Help yourselves."

"This is fantastic, Thanks mate. You're a good Pom," complimented Kenny.

Among the supplies were dehydrated readymade meals called 'Bachelor Browns'. Dozens and dozens of them were carefully loaded on board. But it was later discovered that they were actually revolting to eat finishing with a sickening after taste. They were eventually ceremoniously dumped overboard.

Sam's navigational skills were not required yet. After all you can hardly get lost going downstream on a river can you? In his spare time, he began to gather various aids to help them cross the world. These included a very simple basic radio direction finder, a plastic sextant and an A4 size Olympic school atlas of the world.

"This atlas is great. Look, the countries all have different colours so we know which don't belong to the Commonwealth," he said proudly thumbing through it.

Quietly down the Thames and on the way

Antipodean was moving nicely downstream with its main mast strapped on deck. But in less than half a mile, the motor started leaking oil into the bilges. Within minutes, the whole bottom of the boat was awash with oil. The crew was dumbfounded. All eyes turned to Kenny.

"Kenny, this is becoming a fucking joke," said Kiwi Ted. "I'm sick of oil lapping around my ankles. How the fuck are we going to sail across the Pacific?"

"Okay guys, give me a minute. A few minutes later, Kenny stuck his head out of the cabin. "It's just a corroded washer that's causing the leak. Don't worry, I'll get it sorted."

Kenny quickly replaced it and the next couple of hours were spent cleaning up. After all the boys had had plenty of experience at this sort of thing.

The plan was to return to the roll-on, roll-off terminal at North Greenwich just under 12 miles downstream. Their mate at the office had promised the use of the crane to step the mast.

It started to rain but this was an important day. Up went the sails, the mizzen and the jib. The yacht started to move forward. It leaned over and began to race ahead.

Pride swelled in the sailors' chests. The six of them stood on deck, smiling. Life was good. About a mile downstream a police launch pulled alongside.

"Where are you boys going?" the leading officer yelled.

"We're off to Aussie, mate."

"No kidding. I'm sure we'll read about you," he replied.

The yacht sailed on, down into the Blackwall Reach passing the most famous vistas of London – beautiful buildings against a backdrop of vast parkland.

The mast finally stepped into position at North Grenwich

True to his word, their mate at North Greenwich organised the crane and the mast was expertly and quickly stepped into position.

Then he asked them all to gather around, "Have you had a good trip, downstream?"

"No problems."

"Are you sure?"

"Yeah, why what's the problem?"

"You bloody idiots," he said. "It's very un-yachting to have old car tyres hanging over the side when you are motoring or sailing."

Antipodean had arrived with its fenders still over the side. Kaffir was embarrassed.

"I'm sorry. We won't be doing that again, will we boys?" he said, glaring at the assembled crew. There was silence.

Farewells were made. The old seafaring manager stood aside with a tear in his eye. "I wish I was coming with you," he said. "God speed. Now get the hell out of here!"

South of North Greenwich the docks continued as industry intermingled with old houses and many jetties jutting out into the river.

Everyone was on deck taking in the changing scenery and the ambience.

Antipodean sailed on past Erith as the river began to steadily widen. At Dartford on the south side, the scenery became hilly with salt marshes encroaching into the river. Then, there were more jetties. At the end of one was moored the British training ship, *Worcester*.

"Maybe we should have enlisted and spent some time on that," mused Ted the Dart.

Tilbury Docks, 26 miles from London came into view and then *Antipodean* glided past the Coalhouse and Shornmead forts which faced each other across the river. Shornmead Fort lay in total ruin, its empty gun emplacements alone amongst the marshes.

Progress down the river had been good and they made the open spaces of the Thames Estuary, just as darkness was about to set in.

"Sam, we need somewhere to moor for the night. Can you find a suitable anchorage?" Sam looked at the chart that to him, resembled the inside of a chicken. Looking down there was a mass of lines, markings, signs and symbols scattered everywhere.

"There's a spot called Holehaven Point in front of a sea wall on the edge of a place called Canvey Island. Go up the channel on the starboard side of the bay," he instructed proudly. "There's is a little creek called Holehaven Creek that comes out into the estuary and it looks sheltered. We can moor there, no problems."

"I'm impressed. It looks like those navigational lessons are paying dividends," said Kaffir.

Antipodean sailed on. On a narrow path skirting the top of the sea wall, they saw a man walking his dog coming towards them. Suddenly he began shouting and waving his arms vigorously above his head.

"What's that dickhead on about?"

"Dunno, but I think he's saying, don't go there."

"I don't see a problem, do you, Sam?"

"No, keep on course," Sam ordered.

High on the hill above the path was a pub which quickly emptied out when they saw *Antipodean*. With pints in hand the swelling crowd started yelling and waving furiously, so the boys waved back. Everyone was inaudible.

Kiwi Ted led the charge; "You Pommy arseholes, all Pommies are bastards," he chanted. "When did you bastards last have a shower?"

The sailors had a great time, lauding abuse into the wind while their audience continually yelled and waved back. This went on for several minutes. It seemed everyone was having great fun. Suddenly there was an ominous sound.

A dull crunching sound was heard and *Antipodean* shuddered to a halt.

"Shit, Sam, we've gone aground."

"We can't have, I'm telling you we're on the right course."

"It's a fuckin' disaster, Sam," said Mike, looking at the chart. "You've got the wrong bay. We should have gone left up the channel, not right." Everyone looked at each other.

They were high and dry on the notorious Blyth Sands. Halstow and St Mary's marshes looked ominously on in the background. Within two hours, they couldn't see the river. They were grounded with no water within 150 yards. Worse, the boat began listing in the black thick mud, the smell of which was unbearable.

First night out and grounded in the mud

"We're in deep shit. Your navigational skills are a big worry." Mike would not let up. "I told you Sammy, three nights at the navigational course would not be enough to get us across the ocean. Shit, we haven't even made it out of the fuckin' Thames!"

"Calm down, calm down, you two. I vaguely recall reading an article that explained how to manage a disaster like this," said Kaffir. "Gather all the loose timber on-board and we'll use it to strut and make the yacht stable so it doesn't list."

This was done and the anchor positioned into the light breeze.

"There's nothing else we can do now, but wait. Why don't we draw straws and two of us will stay on-board while the others can piss off to the pub?"

"Now you're talking," said Kiwi Ted.

Kaffir and Mike won the right to stay on-board while the others trudged through the mud and up the hill to the pub.

In the pub everyone was laughing and joking about the useless yacht standing up on its keel in the middle of the mud in the Thames Estuary.

"This is bloody embarrassing," said Kiwi Ted who took offence with the comments. Worse, he was getting abusive.

"What the fuck do you pricks know about sailing? You're allergic to soap and allergic to the sun. Fuckin' Poms! You ought to have a wash sometime."

The barman intervened, "Take it easy boys. There are some hard cases that drink in here. Have your drinks on the house. I don't like brawls and I'm sick of having my customers carted off to hospital."

So with that the boys got absolutely drunk.

Four hours later down at the estuary, the wind lifted which forced the timber props to dig in and as a result *Antipodean* began to lean over. If it had gone right over the life of the boat would have ended right there and the adventure doomed. With no hatches on board, it would have simply filled with water in the rising tide and could not have been re-floated.

It was panic stations!

"Mike, take the main halyard and run it out to the opposite side that the boat is leaning and reposition the anchor in the mud. I'll winch the boat upright from the top of the mast with the anchor. The tide chart says it will come in between 1.00am – 2.00am. We'll just have to wait."

Tide charts don't lie and on cue at just after 2.00am *Antipodean* was refloated. Mike and Kaffir flopped into their bunks just as the others drunk, tired and covered in mud, clambered aboard.

The next morning was greeted with sore heads but renewed enthusiasm. *Antipodean* sailed on down the Thames Estuary and soon it was difficult to see either side of the river.

Sam's error was forgotten as he busily put his skills to use by reading the succession of navigation buoys. He would look at the chart, find out where they were and then head off to the next buoy. The process took most of the day, but soon the English Channel and Margate were beckoning.

"I reckon we should moor in Ramsgate Harbour and take stock of things," he said.

Ramsgate Harbour was on the south east corner of England, 35 miles from the French coast and within easy access to the North Sea and the English Channel.

The approach to the marina was from the east via a well-marked buoyed channel and via a yacht tract to the south of the port. There was no indication to wait in the holding ground near the south breakwater, so *Antipodean* sailed merrily in. Ramsgate was a small but busy port with a nice promenade. A few pubs dotted the harbour foreshore. It was high tide and with smooth waters the boat was easily moored inside the sea wall.

At that moment, an elderly distinguished English gentleman wearing a nautical uniform strode towards them. Leaning over the sea wall he asked, "What size is she boys?"

Mike's chest swelled up, "50ft, sir."

"When you were sailing in, I thought you were Chay Blyth," he replied.

"Who's he?" asked the Dart.

"You bloody idiot. He was the first person to sail westwards non-stop around the world against prevailing winds and currents. His 59ft ketch called British Steel was not much longer than ours," Kaffir told him.

"You know your stuff lad. I hope you can sail this one just as well. But, that will cost you exactly £15 moorage fees."

"You're joking," replied Mike.

"Nope, young man, it's £3 for every 10 feet."

"But that's a night's drinking for us."

The moorage fee was paid but from that moment on, whenever they were asked how long the vessel was, the reply was always 30 feet.

The crew headed to the nearest pub but on their return, a shock awaited them. The tide had receded much more than anticipated, but fortunately on this occasion, did not go all the way out. Instead, it left the boat in about a foot of water.

"We're in the shit again," moaned Mike.

"Maybe not! Let's just sit and wait. We don't know what the tide will do and besides, there's nothing else we can do," said Kenny.

The crew were up all night fearful of what might happen. Luckily, the only thing they felt was a bouncing scraping sensation as the boat flirted with the ocean floor.

The next day was clear with a light breeze as *Antipodean* made her way gently around the point at Ramsgate. She headed out into the channel past the White Cliffs of Dover which formed part of the British coastline facing the Strait of Dover and France. On a clear day the cliffs were easily visible from the French coast and were the first or last sight of the UK for travellers.

The cliff face which reached up to 350 feet, owed its striking façade to a composition of chalk accentuated by streaks of black flint. The cliffs were of great symbolic significant to Britain. They faced towards Continental Europe across the narrowest part of the English Channel from where invasions have historically threatened.

"What a magnificent sight," sighed Kenny.

There was a calm sea with about 25 knots of wind. It was great sailing. The boat scooted along nicely past Shakespeare Cliff which was the closest point between England and Europe.

It was mid-day when a squall struck.

"I'm not feeling well," said Kenny heading for the railing.

"Hold on, lads, this is going to be our first storm," said Sam.

The waves of about 40 feet, cropped closely together suddenly came at them. They were vicious. As the bow hit each wave the boat dived down its crest before partly rising and dipping again. She began to shake. Everyone was nervous and scared.

"I think this is it," a frightened Dart exclaimed.

The pitching went on and on for about two hours. Eventually to port loomed Dungeness Headland, dominated by its huge power station built on the largest area of open shingle in Europe. The area measuring 7.5 miles by 3.75 miles had been built up over thousands of years by shingles deposited by the sea. It was all really irrelevant. They forged on.

Over the next four hours, Kiwi Ted did his best to keep everyone's spirits up by telling an endless string of jokes and recounting his conquests. The good, the bad and the mostly ugly!

Rye Harbour was eight miles further on and it offered shelter. The crew were happy to anchor for the night. It had been a horrible nerve wracking six hours during which the novice crew had feared for their lives. Everyone was on a downer. But a big fry up followed by a nap brightened everyone up.

At 2.00am, the yacht started to bounce again. Bump, bump, bump. The dreaded sensation had returned.

"Shit, I don't believe it. We've hit the bottom again," exclaimed The Dart. "This is getting beyond a joke."

The crew were expert now at the art of mooring a boat but when it comes to laying the anchor, well, you learn by your mistakes. They had an anchor off the stern and one off the bow. It could have been the Thames sinking disaster repeated.

As they discovered some months later when they almost hit a bridge in Portugal, the correct way is to have an anchor out off the bow. In this case, both anchors should have been dropped from the bow.

"Let's get the hell out of here," yelled Mike. The engine was quickly started and the boat moved half a mile to deeper water.

The next morning, Sam gathered them all on deck and pointed into the distance.

"Portsmouth's way down there and I reckon the Isle of Wight is that island opposite. We should sail around the island and head further west hugging the coastline until we get to Plymouth." No one disagreed. Sam was determined to earn his stripes as navigator.

It was late afternoon when Portsmouth came into view and a decision had to be made.

"Shall we carry on across the busy shipping lanes?" asked Ted 'the Dart'.

"Well, it's a very clear night and we have a good wind," Kaffir replied. "It might be dangerous but shit, let's go for it."

Antipodean sailed on, following the Island's southern coastline from St Lawrence to beyond Totland Bay. This wild open coastline provided views of the towering chalk cliffs at Freshwater Bay, the famous Needles Rocks and the multi-coloured sandstone cliffs of Alum Bay.

Our inexperienced crew used the lights ahead for guidance. Behind them, the lights on the Isle of Wight twinkled in the distance and then began to disappear. After a short while there was chaos on deck.

"What the fuck is that?" Sam yelled as a huge metal shape virtually jumped out of the water just yards away in front of them. The boys peered over the side.

"Christ, it looks like a submarine!" Mike said. "It's obviously a navigational hazard bouy. Why aren't these things on the chart?"

Sam was embarrassed.

"At least we didn't hit it," he said, trying to make light of another navigational blunder.

While that moment of panic was overcome another soon emerged. There was a loud humming noise in the distance.

"There's something heading our way making a hellava racket," yelled The Dart.

"You know what that is – it's the Calais to Dover hovercraft. But it's zooming towards us on exactly the same course as ours. What's going on?" Kaffir asked.

"Who's meant to give way?" 'The Dart' asked. No one knew. The 'rules of the road on the sea' had yet to be clarified. Our sailors froze. The hovercraft came closer and closer and then suddenly swerved to rocket by just 200 feet away, its horn blaring in the still of the late afternoon.

The hovercraft's wash gave *Antipodean* a good rocking.

Eventually, she laid anchor in the safety of Portsmouth harbour. That night there was much discussion on the near miss.

"Look we've made a lot of mistakes and we've been fuckin' lucky so far," said Kenny chairing the informal meeting. "Our luck can't last forever."

"We expected to make mistakes. No one except Kaffir knows anything about sailing but how come we could nearly collide with a big fuckin' boat, full with tourists and Poms?

The soul searching went on and on as more beer was consumed. Eventually, the reason unfolded.

The boys were drinking their beer from metal cans but Sam was accidently storing his empties next to the compass. This error of judgement put the compass out by about 10 degrees. So, it was agreed in future to put any empty cans below deck in the stern storage compartment.

But this mistake was later to be repeated with dire consequences.

The next port of call was Plymouth. There were many marinas and options for mooring, so the crew opted for a sheltered berth alongside Plymouth's famous and historic Barbican, just a stroll away from the City Centre.

It was mid-afternoon when they finally made shore. The weather was good with plenty of sun and for the next two days the sailors freshened up. Time was mostly spent in the pub listening and chatting with local knowledgeable mariners who passed most of the time spinning yarns about the good old days.

"These bastards are a pain in the arse. They all know much more than us. I reckon it's time to move on," Kenny 'Nice Guy' suggested. "Let's visit the bonded store and get provisions so we can trade them along the way," he said.

"You mean the grog and the fags, don't you?" replied The Dart.

"Yeah."

Provisions were allowed for a 90-day period with a maximum for spirits and cigarettes. Naturally, the sailors bought the maximum allowed – 108 bottles of spirits, 270 cans of beer and 4000 cigarettes. Total cost was £130.

But the crew were not to know that saltwater isn't kind to either aluminium or steel cans. They mostly corroded or rusted from a combination of sea air and salt water. Another problem was they had no way to chill the beer before consuming, except by tying a thin rope around the can and then dangling it as deep as possible overboard. This did not help. The dreams of lazy afternoons sipping cold beer on deck were just that – a dream. By the time they reached the Mediterranean, the contents of the aluminium cans were all flat!

In the early hours of the morning, it was goodbye to Plymouth. Now the challenge was to cross the English Channel to France. For thousands of years, the Channel has been a stretch of sea that's fascinated people. It's a neck of cold, forbidding, unpredictable water which has claimed many a victim.

The crew had always done most of their sailing in daylight, lacking the confidence to sail at night. That experience was about to change. Sam set a course to cross the Channel at right angles to the coast. Now, this was not the correct thing to do. The proper course should have been to go in a straight line directly to their destination and avoid cutting across the busy shipping lanes. They did not to know this.

Night came and then the yacht unexpectedly became becalmed. Worse, a thick murky fog quickly rolled in providing almost zero visibility.

"I can't see a bloody thing, which means no one can see us either," navigator Sam said.

"Dart, get your bugle. Sit on the bow and blow it till daybreak," Kaffir ordered.

"Yeah, but Kaffir, I only know a couple of notes."

"That will do. Just blow the fucking thing!"

So there they were, drifting aimlessly in the wrong direction across one of the major shipping lanes in the world. There was traffic everywhere. Big black shadows like ghosts would loom into view and pass either side within 100 to 200 yards. They had no idea which passing channel they were in or supposed to be in.

"I'm scared shitless. We'll be hit by someone that's for sure," Kenny said.

Meanwhile, the whining of the bugle was getting on everyone's nerves. 'The Dart' was becoming fatigued and the irregular laboured sound made the noise worse.

"Swallow the bugle and have some lessons when we get to Sydney," joked Mike.

Visibility was still almost zero.

"There's no point in us starting the motor, because then we won't hear the sound of the other ships or tankers approaching," Mike whispered.

There was silence on board as everyone listened intently.

"Hold on, what's that noise?" Kiwi Ted yelled in the still of the night.

"It's a propeller churning up water," someone replied.

"I hope their radar's working or else it's everyone overboard," Kaffir said. A huge tanker passed *Antipodean* within 150 yards, its swell rocking the yacht violently.

It was a frightening 12 hours. No one slept. *Antipodean* defied the odds as towering shadows in the night slipped by. Someone was looking after her that night.

As soon as daylight broke, the breeze picked up and it was all hands on deck. *Antipodean* continued under full sail. The plan now was to head south, turn right down the coast of France and find a port.

It was smooth sailing and eventually some beacons to port came into view. *Antipodean* sailed towards a customs boat which had come out of a big estuary to meet them. After pleasantries had been exchanged, the yacht was escorted towards a mooring about 200 yards from what appeared to be a small town. Edible provisions were needed but it would be hard work getting them from shore back to the boat.

"Where the hell are we?" Mike asked.

"I've got no idea," Sam replied.

"Why don't we go ashore and wander around. If worst comes to worst we can head to the town outskirts because these places usually have a signpost telling you the name of the town?" someone suggested.

Everyone crowded into the rubber duck and headed for land.

Wandering up and down the narrow streets it wasn't long before a couple of signs made it clear that they were in Port de Paimpol.

With satisfaction, the name was scribbled down on a piece of paper.

Back on board Sam flicked through the Olympus school atlas, found France and lo and behold, triumphantly found exactly where they were – on the northern coast of Brittany, France.

"This is sort of reverse navigation. I told you it would all be okay," said Sam.

The two Teds' headed back into town to buy bread and other provisions. Everyone wanted to keep moving, so after the supermarket the next stop was the customs office to get clearance to depart.

"Leave this to me," said Kiwi Ted.

"We've got no money on us," he said in broken French, gesturing with his hands. "Our friends will pay when they pick us up."

Antipodean motored to within 100 feet of the customs office housed at the end of the jetty. When the yacht had turned, the Teds leapt into the tender and rowed frantically towards home. The rubber dinghy was quickly secured and provisions and passengers hauled aboard. It was a brilliant execution.

The engine revved into top gear and *Antipodean* headed at full throttle to the estuary entrance. Meanwhile a French customs officer jumped onto aluminium dingy with a large customs sign painted on its side. He fired the outboard and gave chase. It was 'cops and robbers stuff'. He couldn't go as fast as *Antipodean* which had about one knot of speed on him. The two of them snaked across the bay with everyone on deck giving him the fingers and abusing him in poor broken French.

"Let's give 'em a Maori haka."

The crew lined the stern and burst into a woeful rendition of:

Ka Mate Ka Mate!
Ka Ora Ka Ora!
Tene iti ta ngata puhura huru
Nana nei I tiki mai
Whakawhiti te ra
A upane ka upane
A upane kaupane whiti te ra!
Hi!

With tears of laughter they leapt in the air and waved good bye.

Eventually, they drew ahead. The perfect runner had been superbly executed. Their first on the high seas!

Now it was time to cross the dreaded Bay of Biscay, renowned as one of the most dangerous stretches of water in the world. To sailors, it is known as 'the valley of death'. Many hundreds of boats and ships are asleep in 'Davy Jones's locker'. More than 65 U boats were sunk by the RAF during the Second World War and their wrecks never found.

The day was fine and calm with a good wind and progress was good. About half way across, a huge multimillion-dollar yacht passed them.

"It must be heading out into the middle of the Atlantic because its course is 20 to 30 degrees different to ours," Kaffir said.

But, what they didn't know was that the yacht was on the correct course. *Antipodean* was actually heading into the Bay of Biscay, not across it into the Atlantic Ocean and around the tip of Spain as planned.

An old, large bright orange British Rail steel gas bottle was nestling beside the compass. It had thrown the compass out by upwards of 30 degrees. No one had a clue where they were. *Antipodean* was actually making a wide arc towards the French coast.

Mike and Sam started to have words.

"You know fuck all about navigation," Mike said.

"That's right, but I'm the navigator," Sam retorted.

"This is a joke. It's the second time there's been a huge cock-up. If a storm comes up, we'd all be fucked. Where the hell are we?"

There was silence. Nobody could answer such a logical question.

"Look, the sailing conditions are great. Let's just head in that direction," said Sam wildly swinging his arm to the port side.

On they sailed and at dusk, land could be sighted in the distance. By using the little radio finder they had on board and Morse code signals, the port of Gijon on the top of Spain on the Atlantic was identified.

"You're a lucky man, Sam," said Mike.

"Just good skill, mate. Just good skill!" he repeated.

The boat tied up to the marina close to the centre of town. The mooring fees were really cheap and like most places, there was a visitors' wharf where sailors could stay for two to three days and reap the benefit of a nice hot shower, a laundromat and excellent toilet facilities for free.

It was time to relax.

On a peninsula that divided the port, the nearby historic fishing village of Cimadevilla with its web of narrow cobblestone streets, dead ends, and small squares, became the hunting ground for somewhere to drink. The pubs were pleased with the patronage, particularly their thirst and skill drinking the local cider. The sailors enjoyed the local ritual of pouring cider from bottles held high overhead into glasses held close to ground level.

The main beach, Playa de San Lorenzo was within walking distance and an ideal place to doze off in the late afternoon sun.

At a small cafe opposite, Mike was introduced to calamari for the first time. They weren't the conventional rings, but were shaped like the modern day McDonald chips. Long and thin.

"This is to die for," he told Kenny 'Nice Guy' and Ted 'The Dart'.

Each day the three of them would adjourn to the café for a cider session and a bucket of calamari. They consumed buckets of them. It became Mike's staple daily diet.

After the third day, it was decided to move on and head for Gibraltar. Everyone was fresh and feeling confident in the boat's ability to handle any crisis. *Antipodean* headed east in freshening winds with the current directly behind her.

Mike and 'The Dart' took the first watch and after they were relieved, the wind increased to a light gale force. It stayed that way for the next 30 hours. The following swells would pick the boat up and she would surf a considerable distance before dropping over the back of the wave. It was exhilarating.

The next morning was greeted with blue clear skies but they soon became becalmed. It stayed that way for the next day and night, so the motor was used to keep moving. Hugging the shore, she slowly crept down towards the coast of Portugal.

It was around 10.00pm when Sam relieved Kaffir on watch.

"I think I'll have a little Pernod before I turn in," Kaffir said. "Would you like one, Sammy? It's no good drinking warm beer."

"Good idea and bring up a can of sardines," he replied.

This was a mistake. The two of them proceeded to get absolutely drunk. They finished the bottle and in the process, consumed four cans of sardines. A lethal mixture, especially when consumed in rough waters and that is exactly what was about to happen.

After midnight, they abandoned their post and stumbled onto their bunks. But, within a couple of hours a big storm blew up. *Antipodean* was bobbing around in a howling gale and high seas under full sail with no one at the helm.

It wasn't long before there was mass panic on board.

Sam rushed on deck and pulled the sails down and then proceeded to spew into the ocean. Sea sickness in a storm is tough on the body and mind and not helped by a mixture of Pernod and sardines. This was to be the mother of storms.

Only Kenny avoided sea sickness and thankfully took control of the tiller for three hours while the other five hung over the side.

The gale pushed them along nicely and soon they left the Bay of Biscay behind and were heading down along the coast of Portugal. This was all very well, but they had no idea where they were. Small fishing villages passed in the distance. It was getting all too much.

Kiwi Ted was pissing everyone off, devouring twice his share of food and his chain smoking resulted in him using the last match on board.

"Shit, Ted, we're lost at sea and now the bloody stove can't be lit," a furious Kaffir bellowed.

"Look guys, I'm sorry but I did drop one live match in the cabin."

Everyone got down on their hands and knees and began a methodical search. After an hour or so, 'The Dart' triumphantly held the match aloft. With great concentration and with tension mounting the stove was lit, turned to low and then foolishly left on until the gas ran out.

The following day late in the afternoon, *Antipodean* came across a string of fishing buoys which obviously belonged to a professional fisherman.

"Hey," said Mike. "I bet there'd be some wonderful delicacies hanging off that line. I reckon we haul it in and help ourselves."

"You can't do that," Kiwi Ted said unexpectedly. "It's someone's livelihood."

"Bull shit, Ted. This is not like you. Let's pull the line in," countered Kaffir.

The strain of the last few days began to fracture the camaraderie of the crew as a lively debate followed, before Kaffir and Mike got their way and began the task of hauling in fathoms of line with their bare hands. But it was an uneasy peace. As the coils of heavy nylon grew on deck, the others kept complaining.

"I'll swear that's a gun boat coming," yelled Kiwi Ted peering into the distance. "I don't want to end up in jail so let's get the hell out of here."

Disappointed with the attitude of their shipmates, the line was reluctantly fed overboard.

"You're all cowards but I suppose it's the right thing to do," said Kaffir, determined to have the last word.

The next two days were spent with *Antipodean* sailing aimlessly in the open sea. Finally Kenny suggested, "We should creep closer to the shoreline and find somewhere to check our position."

After a while he pointed, "There's a place over there."

The sails were dropped and *Antipodean* motored into a small Portuguese fishing port identified on the jetty as Viana. This once famous wine exporting port was guarded by an ancient fort which stretched along the northern bank of the River Lima Estuary.

The first thing to do was refill the gas bottle which was easily done at the port general office.

News of their arrival spread fast and before long many of the locals arrived and crowded around the boat for a look. It was not a pretty sight – Sam and Kiwi Ted with their big unkempt blond afros and everyone stinking to high heaven. The boys immediately hit the local café and soon had drunk far too much. Voices grew louder, the locals abused and passing girls invited to 'show us your tits' or 'get ya gear off'.

Near to the cafe was the local police station which was flying what appeared to be a welcome flag on their building.

"We should have a courtesy flag of our own," Kaffir said.

"Yeah, there's a Portuguese one hanging in the port office," Ted said. "I reckon we should acquire it."

Kiwi Ted started a diversion by wrestling 'The Dart' on the sidewalk outside the office. The others cornered the port manager while Kaffir stood on a chair and tried to jerk the flag off the wall. In the distance the wailing of a siren could be heard. The locals looked on not used to tourists, particularly the bad, vulgar behaviour of these visitors. The flag in the port office would not budge. Meanwhile the police moved in grabbing the Teds' who were sprawled on the footpath. The police wasted no time and escorted the crew to the jetty and pointed to the open sea.

There was no choice but to move on.

It was smooth sailing. The water was clean and clear. So clear that on one occasion during a becalmed period, they could see the reflection of the boat in the water. Moments like this were to be treasured.

The old-fashioned seaside resort and fishing port of Figueira da Foz passed them by and with no wind; they motored on for the next 18 hours. Just as they identified the bright lights of Lisbon, a heavy fog started to roll in. So it was decided to spend the night moored just inside the harbour. On a headland at the north-western end of the bight, the warning fog horn of the Cabo Raso lighthouse was blaring out to warn vessels of danger.

Suddenly, the wind sprang up clearing the fog and *Antipodean* increased speed across the bay. "Let's reap the benefit of this wind and keep sailing. The hassle and formalities to moor are just not worth the trouble," suggested Mike.

They sailed on, but in a couple of hours were lost again. Mike and Sam began to argue. Tensions grew. It's true to say that Sam should have completed his navigational course instead of abandoning it after three nights for the pleasures of the pub. But in reality, Mike knew as much about navigation as Sam did.

"Listen you arseholes, we're sick to death of you two arguing day and night. The pair of you are as stubborn as a couple of mules and the truth is, that neither of you know fuck all about navigation," counselled Kaffir.

A frosty truce was made.

The Oriana comes into view

Later that day, a huge passenger liner could be seen in the distance coming towards them. It was the *Oriana,* the largest of the P & O line which cruised between Sydney and Southampton. *Antipodean* sailed over and Ted began waving his New Zealand flag. The passengers who lined the railings waved back. Then, all six crew dropped their shorts and gave the ship a big brown eye. The *Oriana* gracefully moved on.

"We need to know where we are," Kaffir queried Sam.

"Let's go and ask those Portuguese fishermen over there," Sam replied, watching two men hauling in a long fishing line.

Antipodean sailed alongside the fishing boat and a map of Portugal in the school atlas was shown to them.

"Where are we, mate?" 'The Dart' asked.

The fisherman pointed to the map and grinned gesturing to the coast. They were 80 miles south of Lisbon opposite Sines, a county located at the very centre of the south-western Portuguese coast. They were essentially half way to Cabo de St Vincente at the tip of Portugal, the south western most point in Europe.

"Fantastic. Please accept some cigarettes," Kenny offered.

In exchange, the two fishermen grappled with a large European barracuda and held it up. It was more than five feet long and almost a foot in width. The body was long, fairly compressed and covered with small, smooth scales. Like sharks, Southern Hemisphere barracudas are vicious and are dangerous to humans. But in northern waters they are caught as food or game fish. They have a strong taste like tuna or salmon and are often cut up and eaten as a fillet steak.

"I think it's a barracuda but in New Zealand this fish species is full of bones and can have worms," said Kaffir.

The skipper gestured moving his hands like a knife and fork indicating that it was a really great fish to eat. The fish was accepted with some apprehension and flopped and secured onto the deck of *Antipodean*.

He was right. It was scaled, cut up into large chunks and cooked. The northern hemisphere version was delicious. It was the best meal the boys had eaten since leaving London.

The next stop was Portimao, about 14 miles from Lagos in the Algarve region just around the southern tip of Portugal. It was an unattractive fishing port on the banks of the silt clogged River Arade. But this was more like it. At last, the reliable Mediterranean climate with glorious warm days, light winds and plenty of pleasure craft visible in every direction.

They anchored half a mile up the river just as darkness began to fall. A local guide rowed out and explained to them how to moor in the river.

"A line fore and aft from the bow," he instructed in broken bad English.

"What's he on about?" queried The Dart. The guide repeated the instruction.

But our sailors just didn't quite grasp what he was trying to say. "Ignore those instructions we'll do it our way," Kaffir ordered. So they moored a line from the bow and another from

71

the stern. The frustrated river guide left, wildly gesticulating with his arms leaving the boat incorrectly moored on the high tide river.

The usual procedure was followed when calling at a new port – off to the nearest café for too many beers before returning to the boat.

The hot balmy night was a welcome change so Kaffir decided to sleep on deck. He was awakened half way through the night with the sensation that he was moving. Peering around that was exactly the case. *Antipodean* was moving sideways down the river straight towards a low bridge. Lower than the one encountered on the River Thames.

Once again it was panic stations on board.

"Wake up, you bastards, we're in the shit," Kaffir yelled.

Kenny Nice Guy and Mike took up positions on either side of the boat and used their feet to stop *Antipodean* crashing into the other moored yachts. The boat continued to drift downstream. The two Teds' took control of the motor and it fired up about 120 yards from the bridge.

Antipodean under motor, manoeuvred its way back upstream, laid anchor as the guide had instructed and another drama was overcome. Wisely Sam stayed up on watch for the rest of the night.

The next morning, the boys were up bright and early and set sail for Morocco destination Tangiers 175 miles away. The sail across the Straits of Gibraltar was breathtaking. *Antipodean* sped along with a tail wind, surfing the big smooth rolling swells. There were no white caps for miles and occasionally the bow would lift to 20 or more feet out of the water then dip into the swell troughs. It was exciting stuff and great time was made to the Port of Tangier.

Up until now, passport control at the various ports had been a formality. Customs would eye the sailors, check their passports and hand them back. But, the port customs officer in Tangiers got very agitated. He came aboard and then started to yell and began pointing up to the spreaders where a courtesy flag would normally fly.

"I think he's pissed off because we don't have the Moroccan courtesy flag flying," said Mike.

Courtesy flags are important when you are the cruising guest at a foreign port. It is a matter of diplomacy and savoir-faire, to honour the host country by flying their national flag. In doing so, it is likely the gesture will gain a little more visa time to stay.

"It's not flying because we don't have one," someone murmured. "In fact we don't have any courtesy flags at all."

The customs officer motored back to shore.

"This place can be a bit of a dodgy. I reckon we should do the right thing and at least make one to keep these guys happy," suggested The Dart.

The solution was not too difficult. Ted 'The Dart' donated his rather oversize green face flannel and some red electrical tape was found. Kenny Nice Guy then carefully cut and stuck layers of the red tape all over the flannel leaving just the shape of a five-pointed star in the centre. With two holes pierced in the side, it became the Moroccan courtesy flag and was hoisted to its correct position just below the first spreaders at the top of the main mast.

Antipodean tied up at the wharf and this time the customs officer looked up, smiled and approved their stay. If only he had known!

"Bloody dickhead," said Kiwi Ted.

As they were mulling over their next move they noticed a little Moroccan boy hanging around the pier and staring at the boat.

"I think he wants to be the watch boy while we go into town," Kaffir said.

"I don't trust fuckin' Arabs," Kiwi Ted responded. "Fuck off, mate."

It was agreed that 'The Dart' and Mike who were the designated cooks for the night get provisions, while the others stayed on board. Fresh fruit, vegetables, bread and what appeared to be fresh meat were bought at the market. Later that night, the meat was cooked.

"Shit, what's this? It's chewy, tough and inedible," someone asked.

"It could be rat, dog or cat," Dart the cook responded. Although it was their first meat dish for a couple of weeks it was cautiously consumed. They never found out what sort of meat it was so its source of protein was never ascertained!

The water tanks were topped up, gas bottle filled and diesel fuel purchased. Still wary of the Arabs, it was decided not to stay overnight dockside and instead, anchor in a small bay and have a restful night.

But instead of rest there was trouble.

When darkness fell, a flotilla of Arabs rowed out to the yacht with the presumed intention of going aboard and stealing what they could.

"The bastards," said Kiwi Ted. "It's time for some action."

"Yep. Grab the spear gun," Kaffir yelled below.

Everyone had a turn at watch during the night and whenever the Arabs silently approached in their rowing boats the spear gun would be rattled, so it sounded like a gun being loaded. This did the trick and with relief, the night passed without further incident.

The lay time was also used to affect repairs. The crossing from the Thames Estuary to Tangiers had particularly taken its toll on the sails. The usual practice had been to use a needle and thread to repair rips and tears, but besides being tedious and slow, it was impossible to keep up with the holes that regularly appeared.

Mike had a solution. Cut a piece of spare canvas, put contact glue around the edges and press it into position over the offending tear on the sail. This worked well. The downside was that the sails were covered in large and small brown patches.

It was not a good look for the trip across to Gibraltar the following day.

It was now mid-August 1973.

Antipodean crossed the narrow stretch of water to Gibraltar with its yellow quarantine flag flying. The Rock of Gibraltar, a 1,500 feet boulder – one of the Pillars of Hercules in Greek mythology – loomed ominously in the distance. 'Gib', as the locals call it, was governed by the British and being English properly drawn pints were pulled in the 40 or so pubs that nestled on or around its main street.

Europe's only wild monkeys known as the Barbary Apes, roam at will in the upper reaches of the rock's nature reserve.

Gibraltar's runway was the shortest in the world and crossed the main road that lead into town. Traffic and pedestrians were continually halted to allow aircraft to take off and land. Much of town life revolved around Casemates Square, a broad plaza in the centre of the main street, an area that was to become home for the *Antipodean* crew on its two separate visits.

She sailed into the small but extremely busy marina and tied up. A customs officer strolled down the jetty towards them. He was not in a good mood.

"Okay, where are the drugs?" were his opening remarks from dockside.

"We don't do drugs, only booze," quipped Sam.

"I've seen your sort before. You think you can just sail in here and smoke yourselves stupid. I'm not going to allow it."

A heated discussion began. He was absolutely convinced that there were drugs on board and there was nothing that anyone could say to convince him otherwise.

"This is your last chance," he said, pointing his finger up towards the top of The Rock.

"You boys will end up there. It's the castle jail so you might as well tell me where the drugs are and make it easy on yourselves."

The crew were getting nervous. Fuming, the customs officer came aboard and continued to lecture them about the fate of drug smugglers. By this time, another officer had arrived and looked quietly on. After a few minutes he spoke up, "I've made a decision. We're going to search the boat until we find what you're hiding."

With that, the two of them proceeded to pull the boat apart. Off came panels, linings, the bunks were stripped, the galley was pulled apart, nothing was left untouched.

"You're wrecking our fucking boat," Kiwi Ted yelled at them.

"Shut up. Who's your captain?" the officer asked.

Now this was something that no one had thought about. Who needs a captain when you have six mates working together and making decisions by mutual agreement? The six of them huddled together. "Kaffir, you're the youngest. You're elected Captain."

Captain Brian (Kaffir) Muir

"Shit, that means I'm the wanker who has to deal with all the paper work I don't understand, every time we hit port," Kaffir said.

"Exactly! We need someone and it's you," the others chuckled.

"Yeah, well, thanks a lot."

With that, Kaffir went below decks to watch the custom officers continue to prise off the interior. In frustration he began antagonizing them.

"You're getting warmer, warmer, colder, colder," he taunted.

This started to annoy the officers, who could see they were getting nowhere. After about an hour one said, "This is absolutely hopeless. What's more, it's the most untidy and disgusting boat that I've ever seen tie up in this harbour!"

The stench of soiled, unwashed clothes lying around or heaped on top of each other in the sleeping quarters had finally got to them.

"Let's get out of here. But we'll be back!" With that the officers left shaking their heads.

The boys stayed in Gibraltar for a couple of days. Time was spent making good the damage caused by customs and checking out the pubs that were on every corner sometimes side by side.

Limited downtime was also spent sailing around to the other side of Gibraltar into the Mediterranean to some really nice beaches. The weather was hot with tremendous afternoon breezes and the beaches inviting, with plenty of English girls lying around in skimpy bikinis sun bathing.

In one of the pubs they got to know the local DJ. "You guys should have a party on your boat," he suggested.

"What a great idea. We should be able to score some crumpet," said Kenny.

"OK, I'll announce it on air a couple of times."

"There's a party tonight on the Antipodean, down at the marina," he announced on 'Radio Gib' during his morning shift.

It was some party! *Antipodean* was packed with girls who outnumbered the boys 5 to 1. All the crew scored that night. The party also gave the crew the opportunity to meet the locals. One who owned a yacht nearby was to later save Kiwi Ted from a bashing.

One of the problems with *Antipodean* was that she didn't turn about very well. She just couldn't go all the way around, instead would get caught in irons, unable to brace off one way or another, which left her sailing astern. Going backwards was not desirable.

Returning from the beach on the afternoon of the second day with plenty of girls on board, *Antipodean* encountered a British frigate.

"Get out of the way," a voice boomed through a megaphone. *Antipodean* tried to go about, but failed, with the result the frigate had to take fast evasive action. The yacht ended up alongside the naval boat. The sailors were in full uniform lining the side ready for disembarkation procedure.

"I'll show these Pommy pricks a thing or two," said Kiwi Ted.

With that he dropped his Speedos, turned around, put his hands on knees and gave them the Kiwi salute. The girls thought it was hilarious but Ted's bare bum winking at the sailors was the ultimate insult. They were to seek revenge.

The sailors hit town going from pub to pub looking for Kiwi Ted. They could easily distinguish who he was, by his size and huge mop of afro blond hair.

"You boys are okay. We want your mate. We're going to teach him a lesson," they explained to Kaffir in one of the bars. Meanwhile Ted was busy ducking in and out of pubs trying to dodge them, while the others bought his pursuers drinks. This cat and mouse race went on for some hours before Ted returned to the marina and sensibly sought refuge with the owner of the yacht that he had met the night before.

Fortunately for all concerned, the frigate left early the next day.

"Ted, you cost us a bloody fortune last night," said Captain Kaffir.

"Yeah but wasn't it fun."

Eventually the boat was back in order and provisioned so it was agreed the next stop should be the small tourist island of Ibiza, 435 miles into the Mediterranean. Just before they left an English sailor tied up opposite at the marina called out.

"Where are you from and where are you going?" he asked.

"We sailed down from England and we're off to Aussie," Kaffir replied. "We're having a trial run around the Med before we head south."

"What in that? You must be joking!" was the answer.

This was to be a recurring theme during *Antipodean's* life at sea.

It was a calm passage towards Ibiza with clear blue skies and a good breeze which tended to die quickly in the early afternoons. Under motor for the next 18 hours, it bought a bonus or two. A school of small whales joined them a couple of times and large turtles swam along with the boat. Everyday schools of porpoises would follow, ducking and diving alongside. A flying fish landed on the deck before slithering overboard. Under the hot sun, it was glorious.

"Hey, one of the things we didn't do in Gib was go to the laundromat and wash our clothes. Kiwi Ted, you smell like dog shit," Kenny blurted out of the blue.

"Why don't we lash our clothes together on the end of a long rope and drag them behind the boat, while we sail for a couple of hours. Then pull them in and lay them around the deck to dry?" suggested Mike.

"Bloody brilliant idea," said The Dart.

All the dirty clothes consisting undies, shorts, T-shirts and Sam and Kaffir's duffle coats were laid out in lines on deck. It didn't take long to tie them together and soon four ropes hung overboard with the clothes dancing along behind in the boat's wake.

A few hours later, the lines were hauled in and the clothes scattered around the deck to dry out.

Washing done and drying on deck

"I don't believe it," said Mike sniffing his undies. "They're okay and at last we've achieved something without stuffing it up."

That night, they across a sardine fishing fleet about a mile off the Spanish coast. At the time the yacht's batteries were low so *Antipodean* was under full sail. The fleet's navigational lights flickered in the still of the night and without power *Antipodean* looked like a silent ghost ship.

"This will frighten the shit out of them," said Kiwi Ted.

"Shouldn't we go to port and avoid them?" asked Ted the Dart.

"No, stuff it. There are plenty of gaps. Keep on course," ordered Kaffir.

The small boats did not hear *Antipodean* bearing down on them. She sailed straight through the fishing fleet. The fishermen's shrieks of fear echoed in the still night as the yacht silently past.

"I quite enjoyed that," said Kiwi Ted, grinning from ear to ear.

South of Malaga, they cruised about 100 yards off the Costa del Sol coast passing a near continuous urban conglomeration of high-rise apartments and resorts stretching the length of the shoreline.

Tourists would swim out and chat, women were invited to 'come' aboard and the crew would spend hours swimming in the warm waters. Almeria, Cartagena, Alicante, and Benidorm came and went before they eventually arrived at Ibiza Town, the capital of Ibiza on the south east coast of the island. Built on a promontory jutting into the sea, the old walled city looked spectacular overlooking the east coast of the island and its marina. The island was famous for its night life, endless parties and heavy drinking culture. This was going to be one hell of an adventure!

Antipodean manoeuvred into position at the marina bow first for the simple reason that they had not mastered the art of reversing in stern first, as most yachts do. It wasn't long before the crew hit town and friends were made with all and sundry. Females were accosted at random and invited to a big party and cruise the next day.

By mid-morning the generous offer had the boat crowded with acceptances. The destination was the smallest of the Balearic Islands, Formentera, about seven miles away. Dropping anchor off a deserted beach, it was on for young and old. The tiny island had not seen anything like it before. Tourists shed their clothes and frolicked naked in the warm waters. Everyone fuelled with cheap Spanish red wine paired off.

Eventually, *Antipodean* returned to Ibiza Town and the passengers stumbled off the boat.

Kaffir's eagle eyes always looking for an opportunity observed that there was a dingy about 70 yards off the jetty that had three outboard motors on it.

"They don't need all those," Kaffir told the others. "I think that big one would complement our tender nicely."

Antopodean motored over and when she was about 30 yards away Kaffir dived overboard and swam to the dinghy. Hauling himself aboard he unhooked the motor, slipped into the water and attempted to swim back with it. But its weight took him straight to the bottom! Mike joined him by duck diving to the bottom and then dragging it, bit by bit along the ocean floor back to the boat. It was then secured by a rope and attached to the stern.

"I'm not happy about this," Sam said. "This is theft. We could all end up in jail."

"Let's wait till morning and do a runner with it," Kiwi Ted suggested.

"OK."

It was always a pleasant diversion for early morning walkers to stop and watch the departure of a vessel. The attraction of *Antipodean* was no different and gradually a small group gathered on the elevated promenade.

Kiwi Ted took control and started the motor. With *Antipodean's* bow facing the crowd, he gave the order to slowly reverse out while Mike pulled up the stern mooring line.

"Shit, the mooring line's got tangled in the prop," Mike yelled out.

At that moment, the engine stalled. *Antipodean* was still only 20 yards from the jetty.

"Look out. She's swinging around," screamed Mike.

To the embarrassment of the crew *Antipodean* swung 90° so the stern was facing the jetty. In the clear Mediterranean water, it was obvious to see that there was something clearly hanging under the boat.

"There's something under your boat," someone call out, waving and pointing.

"Stay calm, stay calm everyone," said Kaffir. "Ted, dive over and cut the tangled mooring line free."

"Kiwi Ted dived over and cut the tangled line free of the prop and clambered back aboard.

"It's still there," someone else called.

"Gun the motor and let's get the hell out of here," ordered Captain Kaffir.

The engine roared at full revs and *Antipodean* took off with the stolen outboard bouncing along on top of the water behind her.

It was not a good look and it soon attracted the attention of other yachts, but the crew persevered with its new trophy and high tailed it up the Ibiza coast towards Majorca, 50 miles away.

When land was out of sight, it was hauled aboard.

I think I should take it apart, clean and dry it," said Kenny.

"Nuh, leave it on deck, mate. The sun should dry it out," replied the Dart.

Kenny was right. The outboard quickly corroded and was useless. A few days later, an English mechanic in Palma bought it off them for almost nothing to use as spare parts.

Palma, the largest of the four Balearic Islands was on the south coast of Majorca and was known for its beaches, seasonal climate, culture and traditions.

Its warm climate made it a popular tourist destination all year round. Colourful fishing boats bobbed alongside luxurious yachts. The waterfront was dominated by a spectacular gothic cathedral but most of this went unnoticed as the crew settled into the idyllic tourist destination.

There were plenty of bars and girls and it was these pursuits that occupied everyone's mind and leisure time. In one of the bars, a barman suggested that they sail over to S'Arenal about 13 miles across the bay.

"It's full of Pommy and German chicks looking for action," he explained.

Our heroes needed no further incentive. Kaffir called a meeting.

"Look, summer's running out and I can't see the point trying to get to Greece now. I reckon we should see the summer out here somewhere."

"Yeah, but where?" asked The Dart.

"Well, this S'Arenal place is meant to be chocker full of talent, bars and supposed to be cheap," said Mike.

"They say the sailing is good too," chipped in Sam.

"OK, let's do it."

S'Arenal became their new home for the next three weeks. It was near Palma airport and had the greatest concentration of hotels on Majorca and the entire Mediterranean coast. The resort edged along the 2½ mile long and 60 yard wide beach on the eastern end of the bay. Everything in S'Arenal revolved around tourism and leisure with a wide range of bars, restaurants and nightclubs.

During the months of summer, particularly July and August, thousands of visitors flocked there, mostly Germans, to enjoy the beach during the day and to take advantage of the lively nightlife after sunset. The nerve centre was a wide promenade that ran along the entire stretch of the beach. Open air beer gardens and a row of popular outdoor bars numbered from one to 15 serviced the beach and the side walk. 'Number six' was adopted as the crew's home base and starting point for a vigorous nightlife.

It was party time, day and night. Kiwi Ted continually got drunk and aggressive in the bars and was either chucked out or spent the night in jail. The others reaped the benefit of the cheap package tours, packed with Swedish, German and English girls that came and went every day. The boys were falling in and out of love every 48 hours. This was the life!

One of Kiwi Ted's great tricks was to wait until lots of tourists with snorkels and goggles swam out to look at the yacht. As they ducked and dived around the hull, he would present himself in the toilet and lay the biggest turds he could, then pump them out. Back on deck, he would peer overboard and took immense evil pleasure in watching them float towards the divers who to say the least were not impressed.

One day, the crew met a Dutchman called Jon who owned a charter boat. His girlfriend worked in one of the major hotels arranging fishing and yachting day trips.

"Why don't I get her to put you on the hotel books?" Jon suggested. "It will be a great way to kill some time in the afternoons and earn you some extra money."

By now the cost of living was becoming an issue and any venture to get some beer money was welcomed.

"Yeah, let's give it a go."

After a few days, an overnight tourist charter was organised and Jon joined Kaffir aboard to show him the ropes. It was nice watching everyone chatting away and getting to know each other. Some lolled on deck; others had their cameras out snapping the coastline. Things were going well.

"What's that in the water?" someone asked after a while, peering over the side.

The tourists had spotted a large turtle floating on the surface. Jon turned to Kaffir and said, "If we can get that shell, we can sell it for a fortune."

"I think it's sleeping," Kaffir said, "so it should be an easy catch."

Everyone leant over the side with cameras clicking away. The turtle was hauled aboard but as soon as it hit the deck, it broke up spewing guts and flesh across the deck and into the cockpit.

It was rotten. Within moments, the smell became unbearable. The tourists huddled together in groups complaining to each other. Despite cleaning the deck and inside the cockpit, the smell did not to go away. For the next 12 hours the stench became excruciating and many of the tourists vomited over the side.

As darkness fell a huge ship loomed up directly in front of them. As they drew close, the skipper began yelling in Spanish through a loudspeaker.

"Shit, something's wrong," Kaffir said, as the tourists looked on terror stricken.

"Yeah," said Jon. "It's a bloody minesweeper!"

It had a paravane, a torpedo shaped device towed from the bow designed so that its descending cables cut the anchors of any moored mines. There was panic on board. The girls were shrieking in terror and generally there was chaos as the minesweeper swept down on them.

"Just swing her to port and pray," yelled Jon.

Kaffir managed to tack quickly with the minesweeper's paravane missing them by a matter of yards. The wash of the minesweeper rocked *Antipodean* vigorously. Everybody had had enough. It was back to S'Arenal where the dishevelled tour group disembarked and immediately headed to the hotel to complain.

Kaffir's days as a charter boat skipper were over.

With money tight, ideas were floated on how best to finance the rest of their stay.

"Let's start selling our bonded stores of grog and cigarettes," suggested Mike.

"That's illegal. Isn't that for our own consumption?" asked The Dart.

The original idea to finance the trip across the Pacific was to smuggle the spirits and cigarettes into ports along the way and sell them.

"No one wants to work so what better time than now to start flogging off our bonded store," said Kenny.

The bar owners always said 'yes', when they were offered the illegal booty. The usual ploy was to sell three or four bottles of spirits and a few cartons of cigarettes. This generated enough income to buy food and beer for a couple of days.

On a regular basis in the middle of the night, they would also motor into a nearby small marina and steal fresh water from the harbour side tank. As soon as the marina manager or security guards started running down the pier towards them, *Antipodean* would quickly motor away.

One day the manager saw them on the promenade. "You're bloody pirates," he accused them. The crew did not stop to argue the point.

Bad rumours about *Antipodean's* crew were getting around town fast so a new anchorage in the bay about 55 yards off a nearby headland was secured. The water was deep blue and so clear that you could see the ocean floor. It was breathtaking watching the shoals of small fish and the changing reflections in the water. From the new berth, it was easy to row the inflatable dinghy to shore and hit the bars.

The supply of women did not let up. Every day they would swim out to the yacht and scream, "Can you take us for a sail?"

"Of course, we can," was the unanimous response.

"How much do you charge?"

"Nothing, darling. Just come in your bikini and be prepared to take it off."

One afternoon *Antipodean* took about 30 people out for a sail around the harbour. Kiwi Ted's job was to observe the echo sounder and check the depth of water. If it was more than a couple of yards it was okay.

But, he was occupied practicing his bad Spanish on an unsuspecting target. Crunch! The boat suddenly pitched up on some rocks covered with seaweed and jammed. The crew had run the boat aground so many times they were now experts at devising ways to free it.

"I want the boom swung out and everybody to cling to it," Kaffir ordered.

About nine or ten passengers scrambled along the boom, giggling and sliding off into the sea. This scenario went on for more than ten minutes before eight of them were in position.

"Now roll backwards and the hull should lift," he said. On the count of three they lent backwards.

On the first effort, *Antipodean* refused to budge and everyone roared with laughter as the willing helpers tumbled into the sea. New volunteers stepped up to take their place.

"One, two, three, roll."

Antipodean gradually worked her way free and slipped noiselessly back into the water.

Sam also had some fun and games. He would regularly spend the night sleeping in the cradle of various boats to save him the effort of swimming back to *Antipodean* after the others had already returned after a big night out.

One night he won the heart of a little English girl and talked her into spending the night 'on his boat' which happened to be out of the water for repairs.

Early in the morning, he woke to the sounds of men talking.

"Lower, lower. Clamp it there."

He looked up to see a crane hovering above them, getting into position to lift the boat back into the water. Sam wasted no time. He grabbed the sleeping girl's underwear and legged it before swimming back to *Antipodean.* Proudly, he flew her panties and bra from the yard arm.

"Beat that," he said.

It was now the middle of September 1973.

But a light was being switched off. The plane loads of girls dwindled to a trickle. The bars began closing and while the sun still shone, the tourist season had effectively ended. Aimless days were spent sailing or lolling on the beach. To keep themselves amused cans of beer were dropped overboard and then retrieved by duck diving 20 or so feet. There was little else to do.

Within a week, the days began getting colder and as boredom set in hard decisions had to be made.

One Saturday morning, Kaffir suddenly sat bolt upright in his bunk. "I'm going off to the October Munich Beer Festival. Who wants to come?"

There was much excited discussion. Finally it was agreed that Sam and Kiwi Ted should sail the boat back across to Gibraltar for its final Pacific crossing preparation. The other four would go by ferry to Barcelona, collect any mail that had accumulated at Poste Restante and then head for the wild drunken beer halls of Munich.

Kiwi Ted rowed the four of them to shore and waved goodbye as they got into a taxi. But not long after leaving the boat Mike suddenly exclaimed, "I've forgotten my passport!"

"Shit, get back to the boat," the cab driver was ordered.

Mike stripped off to the amusement of dockside on lookers, draped his clothes across the bonnet and swam naked out to the yacht.

After a quick search, Kiwi Ted rowed him back to shore again. He finished dressing in the taxi and they were dropped at the ferry terminal with minutes to spare. But, as they were buying their tickets, Mike realised his passport was missing again!

"Oh no, it's gone forever now. That bloody taxi driver will have it on the black market before sunset," he moaned. He ran out of the terminal. Looking left and right, there was no taxi to be seen. Mike hung his head.

Then there was a tap on his shoulder.

"I think this is yours," a voice said, handing him his passport. The cab driver had found it on the front seat and had done the right thing. Mike never abused a taxi driver again.

The mail run to Barcelona ran into a hiccup on the first night. With no cabins at the camping site the hapless four were contemplating their next move when they started chatting up a couple of Aussie girls. Now these girls were certainly no oil paintings. But what do you do when you urgently need a bed for the night? It was an easy option. Get pissed, do the deed and move on quickly. It was not for Mike and 'The Dart' though who snuggled up under the shelter of the shower block.

"I'm not going back there," Kenny confessed to Kaffir in the morning.

"Shit, they were ugly. Let's go and have a couple of beers," he replied.

It was mid-afternoon when the Aussie girls showed up again. This routine went on for four nights.

Mike and 'The Dart' who now had a cabin were getting bored with their environment.

"Let's get the fuck out of here," 'The Dart' said on the morning of the fifth day. "I've had enough. We should hire a car and head to Munich."

"Agreed! We leave Monday morning."

The four of them had a good hygienic clean up, only to discover that everything was closed for a religious festival until Tuesday. To fill in time plenty of collect calls to the UK were made. The most important was to Highgate where the girls at Woodland Gardens agreed to meet them in Munich.

There was great expectation in the air. But the rail fare to Munich was going to cost £21.00 each – way above their budget.

"Why don't we rent the cheapest car we can find," suggested Kenny. The rest of the day was spent foot slogging it from one car rental firm to the next. Eventually, they had some luck. A BMW sports car needed to be returned to Munich.

Switching drivers every four hours, they arrived in Munich 24 hours later and headed straight for the designated camping ground.

It was crowded with Kiwis and Aussies, some of whom had heard about *The Antipodean*.

"We heard that the boat had been hijacked," someone said. Another said he had heard that it had been sold.

"We thought all you guys were in a French jail. When did the boat sink?" Rumours were rife.

"You'd better get down to the Holbrauhaus. The Highgate girls are there," an acquaintance told them.

Munich's Oktoberfest was justly renowned as the world's biggest piss up. It was a 16-day drinking marathon that strangely started on about the 22 September and ran into the first week or so of October.

Most of the serious drinking took place in 14 beer halls, which had tables and seating for over 100,000 patrons. More than six million litres of beer were consumed while Oomph bands beat out sing-a-long tunes and German ballads. In these drunken beer halls, no one cares. One of the main challenges was to smuggle a signature two litre enamel tankard out of the hall past the security guards.

The boys made their way to the partying Holbrauhaus. The drinking went on and on! It went on until the festival concluded and by then, they were almost all broke. It was an easy decision to cram into the girl's old combi van and head to London.

The beer festival had worked its magic. A few years later, Mike married Sue and Ted 'The Dart' married Donna – two of the girls from their humble beginnings at Woodland Gardens.

Meanwhile, Sam and Kiwi Ted were having fun of their own, albeit of a different kind. As they were preparing the yacht for the trip to Gibraltar, they ran into a friend they had made on their previous stop-over there. He had an ex World War 2 motor torpedo boat and was really proud of it.

As they sat around musing over a few beers, he said, "Look, can you help me out? I've got this mate who I can't get rid of and he needs to get to Gib. He's a good guy and has to get there in the next week or so to pick up another boat."

"Yeah, that's no problem," said Sam. "We could do with another crewman."

The next morning a smartly dressed Algerian in a dark suit, white shirt and colourful tie arrived, carrying an overnight bag and a black attaché case. After some preliminary small talk, he steered the conversation to drugs and began testing Sam and Ted about their attitude and participation in drug taking.

"We just get pissed," Sam said.

"Have a look at this," the man said, flicking open the attaché case. "We can make a huge profit when I sell it in Britain."

"Shit, it's full of drugs!" Ted said.

The brief case was lined with small packets of cocaine. There was an awkward, pregnant silence. Then Ted went berserk, "You black, fuckin' cunt," he said, lunging forward and grabbing the man. Throwing him sideways Ted grabbed the case and hurled it onto the pier. "Fuck off and don't show your face around here or you won't recognise it when you look in the mirror."

"Thanks Ted. I think we should calm our nerves with a quick one," a relieved Sam said as they gathered their thoughts.

After an hour or so in the bar they began chatting to two pale skinned English guys called Derek and Ron.

"You're off the *Antipodean*, aren't you?" they enquired.

"Yeah, that's right," replied Sam. "Why?"

"We're looking for a lift somewhere. Where are you going?" they asked. Sam explained that the next morning they were leaving for Gibraltar and yes, they needed crew to help out.

"You're welcome to join us," Sam said.

"We've never been on a yacht before," one of them said.

"That's alright, we're experienced sailors," Sam replied. "See you in the morning."

The next day the boys set sail, but that night was to be one of terror. Under full sail, a raging storm suddenly struck right up *Antipodean's* backside. The yacht was virtually surfing down huge waves, causing thick white spray to rise over the boat. The four of them struggled to drop the sails as the boat deviated from side to side. Eventually, they managed to get the main sail down.

"The bloody jib won't budge. It's peaking!" yelled Sam.

Despite every effort, the jib refused to move. The yacht continued to surf down the mountainous waves that were capping and then breaking. Suddenly, a wave spewed up in front and the violent force knocked the boat sideways. The wave continued and spun the boat around and then as quickly, spun it back to its original course. As the boat straightened, it picked up speed and its bow dived straight into the water with enormous force.

Then the following wave swamped the boat, the cabin filling quickly with water. The weight of the water slowed the yacht down considerably. Derek and Ron were frightened and continually vomited.

"I don't want to die," wailed Derek. "Mum will go berserk. Tell her I love her."

"Take it easy, Derek. Listen to Sam and we should be okay," Ron said with tears in his eyes.

"Form a line and start bailing," ordered Sam. For the rest of the night they passed a bucket between them, baling out the cabin as the waves continued to push them along.

When morning broke they were exhausted, but *Antipodean* had ridden out the eye of the storm and they had kept the water to a reasonable level in the bilge.

Sam was dazed, tired and had lost his orientation and concentration. Stumbling along the deck, he suddenly slipped and plunged into the Mediterranean Sea. His safety line was fortunately still attached to the rail but he was being dragged along, bobbing up and down in the water out of control, his arms and legs flailing in the air.

There were only a couple of life jackets on board but you couldn't really trust them. They were the old kapok type and were from the P&O cruising ship the *'Arcadia'*, part of the purchase of the useless life raft acquired in Southampton.

"Sam's fallen overboard," yelled Ron above the wind. "Oh my god, what are we going to do?"

"He's still attached to the boat with his safety line," said Ted balancing precariously peering over the side.

"But he's got no life jacket and he's just bouncing along on his back," said Ron, choking back the tears. "Now he's gone under."

"No, there he is," yelled Ted.

The three of them began the laborious and dangerous task of hauling Sam in. Gradually, he came closer and closer. Straddling the deck and leaning dangerously over the side they eventually hauled Sam aboard and carefully laid him on deck. Sam lay exhausted on his back moaning and struggling to breathe as the others recovered their breadth and composure.

"Are you okay, Sam?"

Sam began murmuring in coherently.

"He'll be fine – eventually," said Kiwi Ted. "Just leave him there whimpering for a while."

"Where the hell are we?" Derek asked.

"I've no idea," said Ted. "Ask Sam when he comes to. He's the navigator but he won't have a fucking clue either!"

Antipodean under full sail

The yacht continued to move at a great pace and the North African coastline loomed in the distance. Sam had recovered from his near drowning and the boat was moving along at about 10–15 knots. All everyone wanted to do was to put their feet back on land. A bay emerged on the coastline and *Antipodean* limped in.

It was Oran, a port on the north-western coast of Algeria, some 315 miles from S'Arenal in Majorca. It was located on the Mediterranean Sea about midway between Tangier in Morocco and Algiers, at the point where Algeria is closest to Spain. Oran was Algeria's second largest port with numerous bays either side of it.

They were met by the local customs officer.

"Can I see your passports and visas please?" he asked.

Now it was an agreement on board; never to sail into a port when customs requested you get a visa. This meant questions and the completion of a lot forms. Officials then knew who you were and where you were from. Besides *Antipodean* was not registered!

"We've been battered by a storm and need to make repairs. Can we stay for a day or so?" Sam asked.

"Not without a visa," was the reply.

"Would you like some whisky?" Sam asked.

"That would be very nice. Thank you. You can stay for two days," the customs official replied, taking their passports.

A bottle of spirits would get you anything in that part of the world.

The next few days were spent emptying the boat of water, cleaning, and drying bedding and clothing. The structure of the yacht was still solid and in great shape. Derek and Ron headed for the nearest pub and got paralytic drunk!

Soon it was time to sail the 255 miles to Gibraltar on the southern tip of Spain. "I'll go and get our passports," said Sam

"Can we have our passports back?" he asked the customs officer on duty.

"The police are holding your passports, but I'll make arrangements for someone to drop them back to you."

Two policemen soon arrived at the port and asked Sam why there were no visas in the passports.

"Would you like some whisky?" Sam asked.

"Yes, but my colleague doesn't drink. He would like some cigarettes."

"That's no problem at all."

Antipodean was on her way. The sail to Gibraltar was smooth and uneventful and arrival formalities were completed without any of the hassles of Algeria.

Shortly after they arrived, Derek and Ron secured a berth on a magnificent 60-foot sloop for the trip across the Atlantic to America. Sam and Ted went down to farewell them, "You boys know as much about sailing now as we do," quipped Sam. "If it wasn't for you two guys, we would have probably sunk and died out there," he said.

"It's an experience we will never forget," said Ron. "Good luck for the sail to Australia and New Zealand."

It was now November 1973.

Kaffir, The Dart, Kenny and Mike returned to London to spend the winter replenishing their bank balances. Sam followed shortly after leaving Kiwi Ted in Gibraltar to look after the yacht.

He wasted no time in falling in love with a barmaid at the Capri Bar and spent most of his time drinking there. She lived on an old Dutch barge down in the destroyer pens at the marina, so Ted called that home. He didn't work, just slept until late morning or washed his white jeans to pass the time.

I had spent the summer travelling through Europe in an old Bedford kombi van with Carol and a couple of Spanish hitch hikers we had picked up on the way. Living off the smell of an oil rag, we lived on Crete and then bummed around the Greek Islands, before adopting the very small island of Folegandros as our temporary home.

All good things come to an end and returning to England as winter began, the Bedford van was abandoned in a side street in South Kensington. Friendships were then renewed at Hampstead Rugby Club.

Then, in early November disaster struck. A kick in the side of the head, at the bottom of a rugby ruck on Wormword Scrubs playing fields shattered the retina in my left eye. I spent most of November and December in and out of hospitals recovering from three operations to regain my sight.

It was depressing and Sam would visit me after the pubs closed at 3.00pm. He would sit on the end of the bed and in the warmth of the hospital, promptly nod off to sleep.

"Sam," I said one day. "I'm going off to Cambridge University Hospital to have one last operation to save my sight. If it fails I'll be stuffed in that eye for good. It's the hospital of last resort."

"Shit, that's not good mate. Listen, I'm heading back to Gibraltar. Whatever happens come down and join us on the boat. We'll be sailing for Aussie in July next year."

"Okay."

Waking up in a ward watching people deal with total blindness for the first time was an experience that I'll never forget. They would struggle to find their cutlery, knock over cups or sob in the night. It was not good. My saving grace was Carol who would come up each day by train bringing me sandwiches and decent food. My operation had failed again but I did have one eye left.

Depressed, I returned to London. I got through what was left of December and struggled into the New Year. At night, Carol smuggled me into her room in the nurses' home. But this could not go on. With no work and almost broke, I made the decision to fly to Gibraltar to join Sam and the others.

Meanwhile Kaffir had also returned to the *Antipodean* and wasted no time getting into the swing of things and lots of trouble.

New Year's Eve 1973 was spent on-board *Antipodean*, drinking and generally fooling about, waiting for the midnight fireworks display.

"Stuff the midnight fireworks, I'm going to let off one of those distress flares from the rubber duck," exclaimed a rather inebriated Sam. The flare was stuffed into a bottle, lit carefully and everyone ran for cover. It fizzed away and then appeared to die. Approaching it with apprehension, Sam accidently knocked the bottle over. The flare suddenly sparked and immediately Sam's shirt caught on fire. Slapping his arm with the other and brushing his chest, he yelled to the others, "Help, I'm on fire."

"Your guts are always on fire," muttered Ted.

"Hey, he's not joking," said Kaffir. The two of them began slapping Sam to no avail as he collapsed onto the deck.

"There's only one thing to do," said Ted, as the shirt smouldered. "Chuck him overboard." Sam was dragged to the edge of the yacht and protesting, pushed through the rail into the harbour.

Everyone was roaring with laughter except Sam, who, when eventually back on board, retired to his bunk to prepare for the New Year's Day yacht race.

The New Year's Day, 'Gibraltar All Commers Race' was a blue ribbon event and attracted yachts from all over the Mediterranean. *Antipodean* had been entered and told the organisers that 'for the entry fee we need to cash some traveller's cheques and we'll be back to fix you up'.

"There will be such confusion getting all the yachts organised at the start, no one will check if we have paid," predicted Kaffir.

He was right. The entry fee remained unpaid.

"I don't know about this," Sam said prior to the starter's gun, "*Antipodean* is a big boat and pointing to the wind will move pretty slowly compared to the 20 footers."

"Yeah, but it'll be fun. We'll take plenty of piss and pretend we're not serious," replied Captain Kaffir.

At 2.00pm sharp, all the boats were lined up. The starting gun fired and almost immediately *Antipodean*, under full sail was at the rear of the field. The crew, with cans of Fosters lager in hand, nonchalantly went about their work giving the spectator fleet an impression of 'shit we don't care'.

Sam at the helm during the 'Gibraltar All Commers Race'

Antipodean turned the first buoy in last place but downwind she flew. "Shit, we've a chance," yelled Kiwi Ted.

She picked up the field and rounded the second buoy in third place, but slowed again as the field tacked up wind.

"Wow, what a work out," said Kaffir as they returned to the Marina not disgraced, finishing in the middle of the field. This gave everyone a lot of confidence.

Finding work in Gib was impossible. Sam was working as a part time sign writer and my attempts to find work as a journalist, copywriter, graphic artist or compositor with the local paper and printing company failed, despite a local work permit.

"Sam, you're a life saver. Why don't we head around the coast and try the beaches. If we get work though, you will need to keep an eye on me because after 200 yards I'll sink!"

"Yeah, no probs."

But all the full time life saver jobs had already been snapped up so it was back to square one.

But our luck was about to change. Down the marina on a nicely kept schooner lived a Yorkshire man called Noel.

One morning as he passed he asked, "Are any of you lads' carpenters? I'm the foreman of Fabri Constructions and we've been commissioned to build a new school. I've plenty of Moroccan labourers but can't find qualified carpenters."

"You're in luck. We're all carpenters," said Kaffir.

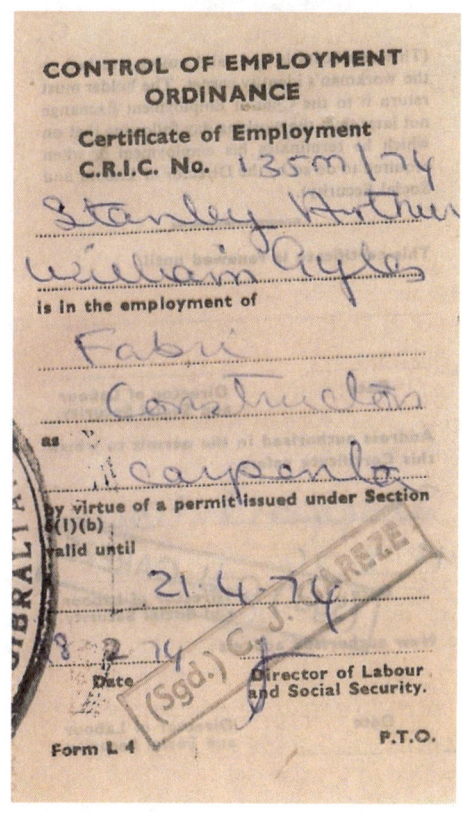

The Auhor's offical work permit to work in Gibraltar as a carpenter

"Thank God for that. It's piece work. The faster you work, the more you will make. Come up to the office tomorrow morning."

"Shit, what are we going to do? We've got no tools," said Sam, as Noel departed.

"No tools and I can't even knock a nail in straight," I said.

"That's okay. You can be the designated foreman of our gang and do the easy stuff and wander around passing out my tools to the others," said Kaffir.

"Sam, you, Stan and Ted go up to the local hardware shop and buy yourselves a hammer and get a set of screw drivers."

The next morning the four crewmen reported for duty. "Where are your tools?" asked Noel.

"They're in London, on the way down here. We've got some basic stuff and we'll share Kaffir's tools until they arrive," said Sam.

"Okay," said Noel.

The rest of the day was spent studying plans – that made no sense at all – and walking through the shell of the school. Noel pointed out shelves that needed to be put up, skirting boards to be positioned and doors to be hung. That night there were celebrations in the 'Corner Bar'.

The Corner Bar was the preferred regular hang out. The Angry Friar and Capri Bars, which were on the wharf were others frequented, but the British navy had the Corner Bar off limits to all personnel. A solid group of Irish would drink something like 'lighter fluid' most of the day and then burst into Irish Republican Army songs at night. It was a rough house with plenty of brawls.

Most nights were spent there. One of the rules the crew adopted was, if you had a spirit, you had to finish the bottle whatever the level was.

The darts room was like a grotto. Cockroaches would hibernate in the dart cases and you had to wait for them to scamper away before starting another game of 'around the clock', or '5-0-1'.

The initiation to the bar was a flaming shot of almost pure alcohol called '151 rum' followed by plenty of beer to cool off. The drinking session to celebrate the new found employment went on for several hours.

"Listen, working on the school will allow us to knock off a lot of stuff to repair and refurbish the boat," said Kaffir. "I think there should be a rule that we smuggle something out every day."

"Yeah, okay," said everyone, nodding in agreement.

"Why don't we also make a rule that if you're out on the piss, you have to come home with something," suggested Kiwi Ted.

Everybody looked at each other.

"Now that's a bloody good idea too."

It was the 6th of January, 1974 which was also Sam's 30th birthday. Five 151 proof rums were lined up on the bar and he was encouraged to scull them in quick succession. Then it was more rum with pint wedgies between. Sam was stumbling all over the place.

"Oh shit, I've had enough. I'm going back to the boat," he mumbled.

Barely able to stand, he somehow got back to the marina. It was 2.00am and the tide was out exposing the lower rungs of the steps from the pier to the boat. Clambering down the steps, the lower rung suddenly snapped under his weight. Lunging sideways in a desperate bid to grab the rail of the boat, he missed completely and plunged into the water, his old black duffle coat weighing him down.

He came up for air but was in trouble. In desperation, he put his arm up and yelled for help just before he sank again. At that moment on the boat next to *Antipodean*, someone appeared on deck unzipping his fly.

"Is anyone there?" the sailor asked with an American accent, urinating in the direction where Sam was. Just as he was about to finish he saw Sam and exclaimed in a shocked voice, "Shit, wow, who man!" He jumped onto *Antipodean* and hauled Sam aboard. Exhausted, he retired for a few hours' kip before his first day as a carpenter. It was a birthday Sam would always remember.

The next night after the first day's work at the school, the crew celebrated again.

It was near midnight when Kaffir said, "There's something I want to knock off from the Capri Bar."

It was a framed picture of the Queen. While no one was watching, he unhooked it off the bar wall. Stuffing it under his jumper he ran back to where the others were contesting a game of 'spot the Pom'.

Suddenly, a voice boomed out, "Hey lad, what have you got there?" It was one of the local policemen, attired like the Bobby's of London.

"It's a picture of my mother."

"Let me have a look at it."

"Are you sure that's your mother. It looks like the Queen to me."

"It's Mum, alright," said Kaffir.

"What? Wearing a tiara and sitting sideways on a horse? Where did you steal that from?"

"I borrowed it from a bar."

"Then let's return it now."

Kaffir led the local plod into five bars claiming he could not remember which one it belonged to.

"I'm sick of this. You're coming down to the station to be charged and jailed."

Kaffir relented and the two of them returned to the Capri Bar.

"Do you want to press charges?" the Bobby asked.

"No. Just get him out of here. I don't want to see him or his mates again. He's trouble and he's barred and so are his mates."

Work on the school continued. It was basic work. Under careful instruction from Kaffir, putting up shelves and louvre window slats was easy and profitable piecework.

The boat's tender was used to undertake sorties at night. We would row around the marina point, load the dinghy up with timber and anything useful and then row back to *Antipodean*.

Noel suggested more than once that we were cowboys and up to no good, but he had no one else to help build the school. He would constantly say, "You should change the name of your boat to Fabri. You've got more of the company's material on there than what's at the school."

In reality, he was right!

The daily routine was the same. The marina had gates at the town end which were manned 24 hours a day by serious glum looking guards who would search the crew's bags. It became a game. Every morning and evening they would ask the same question, "What's in your bags?"

"A dead body," Ted would say.

"A live ferret." Anything ridiculous was said to annoy the guards.

During the afternoon siesta, the Moroccan labourers would meet in one of the partially completed classrooms for prayers. Afterwards, it was a horrible sight watching them lift each other's kaftans and furiously screw each other.

One Saturday morning, Sam and I made our way out to the airport where we had heard that rugby was played on an adjacent tarmac. "Do you boys fancy having a game?" someone asked.

"Who are you?" replied Sam.

"We're the Air Force team. The game starts at 2.00pm and we're playing the Army."

"Okay," said Sam who was an accomplished player in Sydney, "but I'll need some gear."

"We'll fix you up."

At 1.30, Sam disappeared into the change rooms to emerge wearing an Air Force T-shirt and shorts with tags hanging down on either side. The Air Force kicked off and Sam, desperate to make an early impression, immediately tackled the receiver, sending him crashing to the hard tarmac. Within seconds a huge brawl erupted which lasted for about three minutes and the game was abandoned.

"Why did you tackle that Army captain?" he was asked while showering in the Air Force changing room.

"Because that's what you do in rugby."

"No, you are tackled here when someone pulls both tags down on your shorts. That way no one gets injured hitting the airport runway."

It was great entertainment over the next few weeks watching Sam train and play. We would take our girl friends with us, eat and drink the cheap food and duty-free spirits in the mess hall and be the last to leave.

One night after training, the captain approached Sam. "Sam, congratulations! You've been selected in the Gibraltar national team. Be here next Sunday at 9.30am. We travel in an air force jet to Morocco for the annual Cup match."

It was to be a short-lived international career. On his arrival, Sam was bluntly told by the team's manager, "No civilians are allowed on our planes. Sorry." Sam's international career was over before it had even begun.

The simple handyman fixing jobs had now finished at the school and it was hanging doors time. Kaffir did his best, briefing and showing the others how to insert the handles, chisel and position the hinges and push plates and plane the doors so they hung straight and swung true.

Noel handed out the work sheets and my job was to hang a pair of swinging doors midway along a long corridor. Towards the end of the day, I told Noel they were ready for assessment and sign off. Just as he was pushing them to and fro a gust of wind blew up the corridor which acted as a wind tunnel. Both doors crashed to the floor exposing overlapping drill holes, broken bits of match sticks and super glue.

"Stan, it's time you came up to the office for a chat."

I knew this was the end. "You can't sack me, Noel. Please! Look, I'm stony broke and it's the money I earn here that feeds me." I was choking.

"I'll put you on painting duties as we will need to start this in a couple of days."

"Thanks, Noel."

This was a great relief and to celebrate it was decided to have a tequila drink-a-thon after work, at the Corner Bar.

On the command, 'tequila drinkers to the street', the bar would empty and everyone would form a line outside the pub with their hands out. My job was to run along the line fill the small glasses with tequila shots, issue lemon and salt and then stand in the middle of the road and issue the instructions to drink. Then everyone would adjourn inside for ten minutes until the command was made again. The line stretched to 20, sometimes more and the fun went on for most of the night. "Odd numbers, all together, even numbers, girls only, men only." The line became chaos as people began falling all over the road. There were hangovers a plenty the next day.

While the Moroccans were busy screwing themselves stupid at the school, we would usually have a very late breakfast at an Arab restaurant, tucked away above the main street. It was very cheap and the food terrible. Fried bread, eggs, liver and greasy chips cooked in yesterday's fat. But it did put a solid lining on the stomach for the drinking sessions ahead.

Kiwi Ted continued to terrorise all and sundry and began to get worse when his barmaid left to travel Europe. The others were beginning to tire of his drunken antics and only mateship saved his life. Returning home late one night, instead of stepping onto the deck of *Antipodean*, he stepped into the harbour.

"What's that scraping and knocking the side of the boat?" asked Sam waking Kaffir.

"I dunno. It's probably a fender or something. I'll check it out."

"Sam, Stan, its Ted. He's in the drink and struggling."

"Shit, he's blue in the face. I suppose we should haul him out," said Sam. So Ted lived for another day.

Painting the corridor and classroom skirting boards was not proving profitable. It was also tough on the back. Noel had stressed a primer, undercoat, first and second coat and a gloss final coat. Payment was by the finished yard. On hands and knees, it was back breaking work.

"Stuff this, I think I'll go straight to the final gloss coat," I told the others. This went well for a couple of days. Two classrooms and a corridor were completed with just the single coat of paint. On the third day with only a couple of yards remaining on the longest corridor at the school, Noel showed up.

"How's it going Stan?"

"Not bad, thanks Noel. The school's coming along well."

"Why are you painting just the gloss paint?"

"Ohhh, I'm just testing it, Noel."

Noel retreated down the corridor and with his pen knife scraped at the fresh paint.

"Stan, you'd better come up to the office for another chat."

My employment at the school was over and I could see that *Antipodean* was going nowhere fast. I had a feeling that three more months in Gib would not be conducive to my health and hanging around was just not worth it. Besides, I had some trepidation about *Antipodean's* long-term future.

It was time to leave.

The last days in Gib were memorable. A husband and wife arrived in their yacht and moored just down from *Antipodean*. It was easy to observe that the relationship was strained and the wife was keen for sex and easily led astray. It was just a formality to get her aboard *Antipodean* for a cuddle or two.

"Stan, her husband has gone to the police and reported her missing. The place is crawling with cops," said Ted one morning.

"Can I stay here please?" she said. "He'll kill me."

"No way."

Making my way on deck, I screamed, "Get this moll off my boat." This took the police by surprise and with that they escorted her downtown.

I called a meeting.

"Boys, I think I'll go back to the UK and head for the Caribbean and US with Carol. I'll book a return ticket and give the return to Roscoe."

"Sorry to hear that, Stan, but we'll be here till May if you change your mind."

I had just one more thing to do. Break every drinking record in every pub in Gibraltar. The existing records were all recorded on a blackboard behind each bar. At 10.00am on my last day we went from pub to pub. The speed record for the yard of ale and fastest pint was re-written in every pub we went into. I was so drunk that I flaked as soon as I boarded the aircraft.

When I awoke the plane was in darkness and all I could see was the twinkling lights of Heathrow International Terminal, way in the distance. I got off the plane and stumbled up some stairs where the customs entry had been. It had been disbanded and dismantled, so I kept walking – straight into Britain. My meagre possessions were still spinning on the carousel.

Ross Lincoln Seward first met Kaffir at one of the many parties held at Woodland Gardens and was one of the regular bar flies at the City Barge. Their friendship grew when Roscoe met up with Kaffir, 'Kenny Nice Guy', Mike and 'The Dart' at various building sites around London and at the camping ground in Munich some months earlier.

Born in an Army Military Hospital in 1946, he was educated at Takapuna Grammar School, the same school as Kiwi Ted attended. He kept himself fit working as a life guard and participating on the surfing carnival circuit with some success. He completed his apprenticeship as a carpenter in 1969 and later, in 1971 worked in Durban as a shipwright. Possessing this valuable skill, it was natural that Kaffir had suggested to him, "If a spot comes up on the yacht, it's yours."

With this information I sought Roscoe out at a party shortly after my arrival back in London. "The boys in Gib need you. There's a lot of work still to be done on the boat, and your ship building skills are just what they need."

"How will I get there?"

"That's easy. Just use my return air ticket."

"Why are you back?" he asked.

"Because I don't think the yacht will last the distance and I want to stay alive," I replied.

"Bullshit, I'm going," responded Roscoe.

Within a week, Roscoe with a small overnight bag, his tools and travelling under the name of Stanley Gyles arrived in Gibraltar. He was to become the resident cook. With no refrigeration on board, the staple diet over the next eight months consisted of canned food, fish cakes, dehydrated beef, plenty of stew and soups and the remaining horrible cache of Bachelor Browns, given to them by the old guy at The Port of London Authority. To supplement this, Roscoe would seek out fresh vegetables and keep them in a damp sack below deck. He joined the others working diligently on the school and at night continuing the mayhem and mischief.

In keeping with the motto 'never come home without something', Kaffir decided that new batteries for the engine were required.

"Roscoe, we need some new batteries. Let's pinch them off that truck that's always parked across from the runway."

"Okay."

Under the cover of semi-darkness, the two of them slid under the truck and were busy unbolting the batteries when two custom officers approached. One of them tapped Roscoe on the leg.

"And just what do you think you're doing?"

"Shit," murmured Kaffir. "Stay cool and leave this to me."

"We're looking for our pet lizard."

"You're what?"

"He ran under here. Can you give us a hand?"

The custom officers persevered with their questioning as the boys dragged themselves out and to their feet.

"Every minute's vital. We don't want to lose Percy. Help us please. We love him."

It was clear the customs officers didn't believe them but eventually shrugged their shoulders and left.

"We don't want to ever see you hanging around trucks again," one said as they departed.

Later that night Kaffir returned and retrieved his big shifting spanner.

Having another skilled carpenter in the ranks was a bonus for Noel. He turned a blind eye to all the work being done on *Antipodean*. The decks were re-canvassed, a new bowsprit with wire and wooden stays and striping fitted and the bunks and cabin rebuilt or repaired. Roscoe was earning his keep.

Kaffir continued on his thieving exploits. Noticing the port warehouse was unattended; he sneaked in and pillaged two 5kg boxes of liver which he distributed to the other yachts in the marina. This made him popular as favours would be returned.

Another crew member joined up for the 'adventure of a lifetime'.

Peter Robertson had met Kaffir at one of the many London parties and after the friendship grew, had discussed the prospects of joining the crew.

"But I don't know anything about sailing," Peter said.

"Then you are just the person we need."

Pete arrived in Gib in late February. Born in Sydney's Neutral Bay, he attended East Hills Boys High School where he excelled in english and geography; easily passing his HSC exam. He had a background in accountancy and had worked with AMP and various investment companies. In his spare time, he obtained a private pilot's licence and had a job lined up with Ansett Airlines, just as better credentialed pilots were returning from the Vietnam War. Instead, in June 1972, he headed for overseas, spending time in Hong Kong, Asia, before finally settling in Surrey south of London. From there he would go up to Finchley for the endless parties and also toured Europe with the boys in a van called 'The Finchley Fornicators'.

He was of slight wiry build, around 6 foot, clean shaven and in keeping with the fashion of the day, had long hair to his shoulders. He was the fittest and most athletic of the crew. Plenty of swimming had seen to that.

His arrival was surprisingly low key and after the 151 rum initiation at the Corner Bar, promptly got a casual job on a local charter boat.

Not long after his arrival, the police arrived at the dock and went aboard the *Antipodean*.

"We have a guy who's been accused of bringing drugs in from Morocco. We need eight men, 6 feet plus, with long dark hair for a police line-up. Will you volunteer?"

"Yeah, we can help out."

With others selected from the Corner Bar they met up at the police station and lined up in a small narrow room. To their shock the ninth person was short with blond hair and pale white skin.

The accusers came in and were asked, "Which one is he?" Without hesitation, the small blond man was picked out.

"Thanks boys, justice has been done. Anyone like a cup of tea?"

By now it was early March and work at the school was drawing to a close.

Kaffir and Roscoe were contracted to work on the construction of a new sports stadium, putting up concrete formwork. They employed Sam as a labourer for £1 per hour. After the concrete formwork was up, the steel was inserted and then the concrete poured. Sam would then remove the formwork.

Kiwi Ted, shacked up on another boat was almost broke and refused to work while Peter continued with his charter work.

Moored in the marina was a luxury 42 feet catamaran called the 'Solaris Maiden'. Its skipper was an old English gentleman called Malcolm. His crew consisted of a married American couple with a baby. The parents would sleep in until late morning, laze around and did little maintenance on his boat.

Returning from the stadium one afternoon the group saw Malcolm in a distressed state, sobbing with his head in his hands.

"Are you okay, Malcolm? What's wrong?"

"No. Gosh, I've been accused of rape by the married couple. She said I tried to rape her while the husband was in town. I swear it's a put up job. It's just not true."

"Where are they now?"

"They're at the police station making a statement."

"Look, get yourself a local lawyer quick smart, said Kaffir. "If there's anything we can do let us know."

"We'd better look after him," Kaffir told the others. "I reckon he's telling the truth."

Each day the boys called on Malcolm who was panic stricken. He told them that the couple had said that if he paid them £500, they would drop the charges.

"My lawyer has told me I'm in an impossible position and the best thing to do is just leave."

"I think that's the thing to do. The pair of them won't hang around for the trial and we'll make sure the yachting fraternity don't make them welcome. Do a runner."

The following morning, Malcolm approached the boys and asked them if they would crew for him.

"I'll head for Spain tomorrow and hole up."

"Okay, no problem. Where is the family now?"

"Staying on another yacht and using mine as a hotel," Malcolm replied. "All I ask is that you put all their gear onto the quay and don't steal anything. I don't want to upset them. I'll see you at sunrise."

When he left, the crew had a meeting. They all agreed that Malcolm was a fantastic old bloke, but the American couple needed to be taught a lesson. When dawn broke, all the couple's possessions including food was heaped on the quay. Roscoe, Sam, Peter and Kaffir, then proceeded to open all the cans of food, jars of jam and mix the lot into their clothes. The baby's dirty disposable nappies were laid inside their sleeping bags. The bags were then zipped up and left on the quay in the hot searing sun.

"That'll teach those bastards a lesson," said Sam.

Conditions on Malcolm's Cat were fantastic. Everyone had individual cabins with an intercom. The fridge was full with beer and the Cat had all the latest sails, equipment and electronics.

But in their haste to leave they forgot to notify customs they were leaving port. When they realised this they were in the upmarket marina of Puerto Banús in Marbella, Spain on the Costa del Sol. The marina was built just a couple of years before by a local property developer and the lavish opening was attended by, amongst others, the Aga Khan, film director Roman Polanski, Playboy founder Hugh Hefner, Dr. Christian Barnard and Prince Rainier and Princess Grace of Monaco. A youthful Julio Iglesias was contracted to sing for the guests for the enormous sum of 125,000 pesetas. An army of 300 waiters from Seville, served 50 pounds of beluga caviar to the 1,700 guests. It was a place for the jet-set and the super-rich, where all the boat owners go ashore in tuxedos and dine at the exclusive yacht club.

Malcolm would spend a lot of time in a small Spanish bodega where he was known as 'The Millionaire', while the crew lazed around in their Speedo's chatting up girls and drinking beer. After two weeks, it was decided to return to Gib.

"We have to get back without being caught," said Roscoe.

"Shit, how are we going to do that?"

"We go in groups. It's everyman for himself."

Kaffir, Roscoe and Peter went down to Malaga and managed a lift in a large launch. When it arrived at Gib and just before customs came on board they leapt off, ran down the wharf and climbed into their bunks.

"Where are your crew?" customs asked.

"I don't know. They were here. They must have run away," responded the skipper.

Meanwhile Sam was helping a Gibraltarian sail a small yacht across into the marina. Safely in, Sam made his way home and everyone was soon in their bunks.

"Is anyone there? Its customs here," a voice said without warning.

Everyone froze.

"We've had a complaint from some Americans that there are drugs on board."

It was possible that the American couple could have broken into *Antipodean* and planted drugs while the boys were crewing for Malcolm.

"That's impossible. You know us. There are no drugs here."

Everyone was nervous. The custom officers were unsure but continued to question them at length.

"We're sailing this to Australia then New Zealand. As you know we've been working here building your school and sports stadium. We just don't do drugs," Sam explained. With that, the custom officers left.

In the morning Roscoe and Kaffir walked confidently past the marina guard and customs post with their saw bags as if nothing had happened.

The custom officers looked curiously on.

"I wonder what's going through their minds. We've been away for two weeks and they must have noticed that we've not been around," whispered Kaffir.

"I would have thought they would be waiting for us," said Roscoe.

"Just keep walking."

"Shit, that was close. They're confused. We've got away with it," said Kaffir.

The arrival of Gary Dunne, the final new crew member to be assembled, was to liven up activities. He had arrived in the UK in 1972 and had met Mike, Roscoe and Kaffir on the many building sites where employment agencies sent a lot of Aussies and Kiwis. Prior to that, he had been travelling in a small minivan and had met Peter at a camp site in Spain. It was here that he was given the most appropriate nickname of 'Grot'. Everything he did was either rude, ugly or in bad taste. The ultimate pest; the sort of person only a mother would want to own.

Born in Yarraville, Victoria, he finished his education as a boarder at St Vincent's Catholic School in Bendigo, before completing a five-year apprenticeship as an electrical instrument maker. With a big broad strong physique, Grot didn't care much about personal cleanliness or what clothes he wore.

He made a name for himself the moment he boarded the plane at Heathrow for the four hour flight to Gibraltar. Drinking cans of beer non-stop he helped drink the plane dry and then took comfort in sharing a bottle of rum provided by two navy boys seated in front of him.

Sam, Roscoe, Kaffir and Peter met him at the airport.

"Shit, you're pissed out of your head," said Roscoe.

"Yeah, I'm only starting."

"We'd better introduce you straight away to the Corner Bar then," said Roscoe.

"Let's go straight there."

Handing him a flaming rum, Grot sculled it without blowing out the flame. Swaying against the bar, flaming rum dripped down his T-shirt. Thrashing madly, Peter managed to put out the flames, but Grot's lips were blistering quickly.

"Get me a can out of the suitcase," yelled Grot, frantically. The contents of his suitcase were a revelation. It was packed with rows of large cans of Fosters lager beer. The only other thing in it was a towel which was laid across the top.

"Where's the rest of your gear?"

"That's it. It cost me a fortune in excess baggage."

Grot had arrived with no clothes, just a suitcase full of beer just like Barry McKenzie, the legendary Aussie tourist who revealed his suitcase to customs in England a year or so previously. The difference was a movie was made called, *'The Adventures of Barry McKenzie'* which turned out to be a worldwide hit.

The drinking continued until he could hardly stand. Stumbling outside, he collapsed on the narrow footpath.

"What do we do with him now?"

"Leave him in the gutter for the dogs to lick him," someone suggested.

"You guys lug him back to the boat. I'm going to knock off that bike," said Kaffir pointing across the road.

As he mounted the bicycle, there were shouts from a nearby café. Some burly locals emerged and began to give chase as Kaffir took off peddling furiously towards the newly constructed school. As he drew away from his pursuers, he chose a short cut along the sea wall. He began tiring after 200 or so yards and the bike began to get the wobbles. It was all over in a few seconds. Kaffir and the bike tumbled off the raised walkway into the sea. Fortunately, the high tide covered the retaining walls many rocks. Kaffir hauled himself back up onto the walkway and abandoned the bike into the sea.

There were certainly plenty of stories to be told in the morning. The first was when Grot woke up.

"Where the hell am I, is this heaven or is it hell?"

It was now late April and unexpectedly Ted 'The Dart' and Mike arrived in Gibraltar with a big new genoa, a smaller main sail and a spinnaker. The old cotton sails were disposed of and the genoa fitted to the bowsprit. After three days work, everyone was looking forward to an early morning test sail.

It was sensational. The sails easily ballooned and the genoa bent the bowsprit as *Antipodean* leapt ahead at speed out of the marina.

"Wow. We've cracked it. Thanks guys, that's brilliant," said Kaffir.

Satisfied, 'The Dart' and Mike headed back to the UK a few days later.

"Good luck boys. You are going to need it," was The Dart's parting shot.

Life in Gibraltar continued to consist of eating bad food, working at the stadium, drinking and preparing *Antipodean* for the voyage ahead. Three more tedious weeks passed.

One day, on returning from one of the many sea trials around 'The Rock', *Antipodean* passed a naval war ship which was awaiting instruction to enter port. On deck were an Admiral and 200 sailors lining its perimeter, all standing to attention. The ship gave a seven gun salute and in turn, received one from shore.

"Let's check it out," suggested Grot.

Antipodean drew alongside. At that precise moment and without hesitation, Grot gave the crew the 'fingers'.

"You shouldn't have done that Grot," said Sam, relating the story when Kiwi Ted did a similar insulting thing some months earlier. "Listen mate, as soon as we make shore, you've got to disappear until the war ship leaves port," said Sam.

"I think it's time to call in a favour from my liver eating friends further down the pen," Kaffir replied.

Bert, an elderly British solo sailor thought the whole episode was most amusing, and hid Grot in the bowels of his small yacht off shore until the ship left port.

On another occasion, the Royal Navy submarine *HMS Opportune* spent three days in port.

Let's get to know some of the crew and see if we wrangle a way to get on board," suggested Grot.

As some of the crew sauntered past the Corner Bar, they were invited in for a drink or two. This soon opened the door for an invitation to 'join us for drinks on the sub,' which was gratefully accepted. Needless to say the boys hit the duty free spirits and had the sub crew singing bawdy songs and eventually left worse for wear. Staggering back to *Antipodean*, Kaffir exclaimed, "Shit, I forgot to steal something."

"That's okay," said Grot reaching for his pocket. "I've taken care of it."

"Holy Mary, it's the Captain's cap," blurted Roscoe.

In the following months, the boys would take turns at wearing it when ashore in the various ports they would call into.

A meeting was called. It was decided to set sail and spend the summer, sailing the Mediterranean and then in December, cross the Pacific to Sydney, Australia.

But first a ship's bell was needed.

On the boat in the next berth was a bell hanging in the cockpit. Sneaking on board, Kaffir unscrewed it and hid it under the spare sail, stowed aft on the yacht.

No one thought anymore about it, until a few days later a policeman stopped by *Antipodean*.

"There's been a ship's bell stolen from the boat next door. Have you seen anyone nasty around?"

"No sir, we haven't seen anyone, but we'll keep an eye out," replied Kaffir.

"Thanks. There's been a fair bit of petty pilfering going on and we are determined to catch the culprit."

It was time to leave. Kaffir, Sam and Roscoe quit the stadium job much to the disappointment of the Arab boss. In reality they had done a great job, earned good money and it was sad to depart.

It was also crunch time for Kiwi Ted. He was given the facts.

"You've got no money, no skills and we have six crew for five spots. We can't lend you any more money. What do you want to do?"

"Thanks for the ride boys. I'll head back to London."

On Tuesday 28 May 1974 at 10.30am Kaffir, Sam, Roscoe, Peter and Grot set sail from Gibraltar in a moderate easterly wind, of 14–18 knots.

By prior arrangement they agreed to race a big charter sloop called the *'Cosmic Star'* across the 19 mile stretch to Ceuta, a small Spanish owned territory nestling on a peninsular at the northern tip of Morocco in the Straits of Gibraltar.

The bet was simple. The loser provides the dinner plate for all.

Within minutes of motoring to the starting point, Grot committed his first atrocity at sea. Roscoe, who had been appointed chef for the journey had purchased a large bucket to wash the dishes in.

"This is strictly to be kept clean and hygienic," he told the others.

Hearing chuckling below deck, Roscoe peered down into the galley and watched in horror as Grot squatting on the bucket disposed of his greasy café breakfast.

"Oh, shit."

"Yes, literally," Grot smirked.

"You bastard," was all Roscoe could say.

The race started with *Antipodean* under full sail. About half way to Ceuta with the *Cosmic Star* leading, a gale blew up. With a charter on board and in rough waters, she had to drop her sails. With that, *Antipodean* sailed past easily, but the sudden introduction of long high waves with crests breaking into spray, had an immediate effect on Grot. He was over the side, vomiting his heart out much to the amusement of the others.

The fact that *Antipodean* had won did not stop both crews attacking *Antipodean's* bonded store that night. Three bottles of bourbon were drunk. The mood was good.

Then over the sounds of laughter, a huge splash was heard.

Kaffir had continued a re-occurring theme. While stepping from the *Cosmic Star* onto the *Antipodean*, he disappeared vertically into the harbour smashing his Adam's apple on the way down against one of the old tyres which acted as a fender.

In the gentle swell, the two yachts rafted side by side continually nudged against each other.

"Quick, separate the boats and brace them," yelled Mick, the skipper of the *Cosmic Star*.

Three of the crew struggled valiantly to keep the boats apart. Eventually to everyone's relief they hauled Kaffir out of the water. With his swollen throat and jaw, Kaffir retired gracefully to his bunk as the others partied on.

The next afternoon Ceuta and the *Cosmic Star* became a distant memory. *Antipodean* departed and skilfully navigated by Sam, hugged close to the Algerian coast. She was flying along with Sam and Pete cramped in the cockpit. The yacht was proving difficult to steer and in the middle of the night, she broached and occasionally jibed. The boom would come crashing over and *Antipodean* would career off course. It was exciting sailing. In 48 hours they covered almost 400 miles.

The wind dropped and *Antipodean* was becalmed. The new main sail had had its first prolonged buffering and it showed. It was flaying on the stays and some of the stitching had come apart.

"We'd better get it down, Sam. You and Roscoe can do the stitching," ordered Captain Kaffir.

With the main down little progress was made so the spinnaker was put up.

"Shit, she looks good," said Peter as the boat increased its speed to about three knots.

"We should call it something."

From that moment on the spinnaker was to be called Casper after the ghost.

It took Sam and Roscoe seven hours over the next two days to stitch the sail, before it was raised again. Repairs were also done to the sliding track on the boom, but another rip appeared on the main sail. It had to be re-sewed again. *Antipodean* was bobbing up and down on the relatively calm seas.

In the distance, a Greek tanker about 600 metres away did a big U-turn.

"What the fuck does he want?" asked Grot as the tanker came closer.

When it towered over them a voice boomed through a loud speaker in Greek.

"I think they're just checking that we're okay," suggested Peter.

The boys waved from the deck. The tanker gave them three blasts on its horn, turned and moved on.

Little progress was made during the next 18 hours. Roscoe joined Kaffir on duty.

"It doesn't look good. I think a storm's approaching," he advised.

The wind increased to 30 knots and almost immediately the sea turned into high waves with long overhanging crests. Visibility was poor and the surface on the water took on a white appearance.

"Get Grot up here to help get the main sail down. This looks serious."

Roscoe and Grot tried in vain to lower the sail while Kaffir struggled to hold a course on the tiller. The force of the wind and high seas suddenly knocked *Antipodean* down onto her side, the cross-trees plunging in the water. Grot and Roscoe hung grimly onto the mast up to their waists in water with their feet on the toe rail for support.

The sea poured into the hatch like a water fall. The jib cleat was let go and, as it was released the boat popped up into the wind.

"Wow, shit, fuck. What an experience," yelled Grot.

"Yeah, but look at the main sail," said Kaffir. "The stitching's come apart. It's disintegrated."

The big seas did not relent. Mid-afternoon the motor was started and *Antipodean* headed towards the Algerian coast for shelter in a cove. Everything below deck was soaking wet.

Clad in his sardine outfit consisting waterproof long pants, coat and hat, Peter attempted to grab some sleep on his bunk, which was soaking wet. It was hopeless.

Antipodean eventually spent the night sheltered from the wind and angry sea and in the morning it was decided to go ashore.

"Where the fuck are we, Sam?"

"I don't know. These rag heads will know," he replied as two local sullen customs officers motored and came aboard.

They spent over an hour questioning the crew about who they were and why they wanted to spend time in Algeria. At that time, Algeria was in the middle of an independence struggle and had closed all her borders.

Eventually, one acted as pilot and navigated them into a small marina at Sidi Ferdj, which was 15 miles west of Algiers.

"You stay two days and then you leave," they were told.

The crew set about drying clothes, tools, spare sails, in fact anything moveable was spread on deck or on the marina walk way.

Tied up for repairs at Sidi Ferdj, west of Algiers

The local police strolled down to check them out on the hour. This made the crew feel uncomfortable.

The tears and condition of the stitching in the main sail was causing concern.

"We can't continue with this problem. We need to get the main sail professionally mended. I'll ask the cops to take us to a sail maker," said Kaffir.

The police kindly obliged. Kaffir and Sam were escorted into Algiers to a special marina compound that was out of bounds to Algerians. There, two old ladies spent two hours checking the sail and working their magic with a sewing machine. The boys were hung around and then were escorted back.

"Your sail's fixed. Now leave."

"We can't. The bowsprit needs fixing, the genoa needs sewing and the bilge pump is rooted," explained Kaffir.

"You have 24 more hours."

That night in the local café they met three French couples who were really enjoying themselves singing and dancing to hit songs from the 50s and 60s. The crew joined them until the early hours of the morning.

"Why don't you come down early tomorrow and join us for a pre-lunch drinks?" asked Roscoe.

"Sounds good."

Sure enough on time their new friends arrived and another party began.

"It's hard to work out who's with whom," said Peter. "I reckon there're screwing each other." More whisky was drunk.

"We'll shout you all dinner tonight," said one of the French women.

"I can't stand it. I'm going to poke the blond one," Peter said.

After dinner at about 10.00pm Peter led her back to the boat. Grot, already hiding aboard, was waiting for the show to begin. Peter laid her on the engine box slipped her bikini bottom to her ankles, unzipped his shorts and climbed aboard.

"Nice performance, Peter. Now it's my turn."

"No, it's not," Goldilocks said, adjusting her bikini bottom. "I'm going back to the others for more fun."

In the morning, everyone was nursing sore heads. The police returned.

"We've told you we don't want you here. Your time is up. Leave now!"

"You can't make us leave," said Kaffir gesturing. "Under international law we're entitled to seek refuge and stay until the boat is safe to sail."

"Either you leave now, or we'll tow you out to sea."

"Okay, okay. Start the motor and let's get the fuck out of here," Captain Kaffir ordered the crew. With no wind, little progress was made. Everyone sunbathed nude on deck.

Going for the overall tan after the big night

118

Pete's sexual encounter the night before must have been playing on Sam's mind, so he went below deck to the 'wank tank' and then re-emerged on deck.

"Kaffir, while I was in town, I bought you a little bag of sweets," he said. "I know you have a sweet tooth."

"That's nice, Sam. Thanks mate. Pop it down there."

Kaffir tore open the brown paper bag to discover semen streaks instead of lollies.

"That's disgusting, you filthy bastard!"

The next few days were spent doing very little as the easterly wind hindered the yacht's progress. She meandered along. Then a small port identified by Sam as Dellys, about 60 miles east of Algiers, came into view on the port side.

"Let's go in there until a westerly comes up and affect any repairs," suggested Roscoe. It was a struggle to get *Antipodean* moored in the crowded harbour. Twice she glanced off fishing boats, ran aground and continually hit other mooring lines.

"I'm not sure this is a good idea."

"It's okay. Here come some locals to help out."

Two hours later, *Antipodean* finally tied up. Within minutes the harbour police came aboard and began a long and tedious discussion in a mixture of broken English and Algerian Arabic.

"What's in there?" one asked pointing to a stack of cans."

"Sardines."

"I'm going to open two at random."

"Why?"

"They could be filled with drugs."

The crew looked on nervously as the police sampled and then consumed the two tins. With that the police methodically searched the yacht.

"Nice eh?' asked Grot.

"I need to see your captain up in the harbour office."

Kaffir trooped off with the two harbour police who let him know in no uncertain terms, that to stay would cost them two bottles of whisky and 200 cigarettes.

"The bloody ragheads," said Grot. "I feel like taking the top off and then pissing in the whiskey."

"We all do, Grot, but this might be the last port for five or six days."

The time ashore was put to good use. Oil had leaked from the engine and drained into the bilge pump which needed emptying. Roscoe purchased provisions while Sam mended the sails. Grot washed his clothes for the first time.

On Sunday 9 June, a good 25 knot westerly sprung up gusting to 35 knots. The fishing boats left port early in the morning and so did *Antipodean.*

Grot was determined to improve his sailing skills and got the 'sailor of the week' award for bringing down the genoa in the not so impressive time of 25 minutes, 30.42 seconds. First he tried to bring it down out on the bowsprit with the halyard still cleated at the bottom. Then he dropped it into the water, let the halyard go loose with the jib flying aimlessly around. It was a comedy of errors enjoyed by the others.

After a while the weather turned and heavy seas and gusting winds of 40 knots made everything soaking wet again.

On the fourth day after leaving Dellys the wind settled into a south easterly, so for the first time in a week, up went the main sail and genoa.

A Norwegian freighter caught them and began running parallel to the yacht and then suddenly cut across the stern, straightening up directly behind *Antipodean.*

"What are those pricks up to?" asked Grot who was at the helm completely naked. "It's bloody big. Shit, look at the swell that's coming. If we capsize, none of you bastards are having this life jacket I'm using as a cushion," he said.

The waves from the freighter were causing concern on board *Antipodean.*

"I've got no compass, so I don't know where the fuck I'm going," yelled Grot.

"Just try and keep her in a straight line."

The yacht began careering left and right as the huge swell rocked and tossed the boat. Eventually, the freighter continued on its way. Later, Grot was acknowledged with the 'helmsman of the week' award by having to drink half a bottle of bourbon in 60 minutes.

For the next seven days the wind was unpredictable, as *Antipodean* alternated between main sail to sailing under jib and mizzen.

Roscoe and Grot would take turns being towed along behind, holding on to a long rope. It was great fun until Grot, instead of bouncing along on top of the water got dragged under and let go of the rope.

"Shit, Grot's gone," yelled Sam who had been observing them.

"Can anyone see him?" asked a panicking Kaffir.

"No!"

"Shit turnabout and charge the motor."

Everyone leaned over the side peering into the sea, hands cupped to their foreheads. Turning the yacht to where Grot had disappeared was almost impossible.

"There he is!" yelled Peter pointing to a dot about 80 yards away.

Antipodean motored towards him and it became obvious that Grot was in real trouble. He continually went under and then would bob up again and then disappear with the rise and fall of the waves. Getting the yacht into position for the rescue was difficult but eventually they drew alongside. Peter grabbed him and three of them pulled him closer to the boat and then roughly hauled him aboard.

The naked Grot was almost unconscious. He was laid on deck face up; Sam freed his tongue and frantically began CPR. The others looked on. Not a word was spoken as Sam pushed hard down onto his chest.

After around 5 minutes, Grot began spluttering and coughing up sea water.

Gradually he recovered, but was not impressed with the rescue mission.

"You bastards, I could have drowned out there."

"That's what we were hoping for Grot," said Peter grinning.

The plan was to make Tunis the next port of call. A couple of days out, Peter decided to dry his mattress on deck. The day was hot and the sailing trouble free. Everyone was lolling about naked.

Grot decided to take advantage of the comfortable mattress reading a crumbled pornographic magazine. Soon he was quietly moaning, his backside rising up and down. Then without warning, he leapt to his feet, tugged vigorously at his penis and ejaculated all over Peter's mattress.

"Sleep well," he said.

"You dirty bastard!" retorted Peter.

This was the signal for Kaffir to don his leopard skin loin cloth he had made from a table cloth purchased in South Africa as a mother's day gift but had never sent. It was to serve him well as it offered his family jewels protection from the scorching Mediterranean sun.

"It gives me an air of respectability and distinguishes me from you lot," he told the others.

Later the next day, Grot was at the helm again attempting to win successive 'helmsman of the week' awards. Ahead of the yacht was a Russian freighter throwing up a nice following wave in its wake. Grot manoeuvred *Antipodean* towards it and soon she was surfing along merrily behind. Within 10 minutes, the yacht had encroached to 30 feet behind the freighter.

"Swing it, Grot, or we'll hit the bloody thing," said Kaffir desperately.

Steering the boat sideways, *Antipodean* swung alongside and then veered away avoiding yet another potential disaster.

"I was enjoying that."

"No. I think you should retire as helmsman!"

"Give me another chance. I promise I'll tell you if I come within 100 yards of another ship."

"Okay," said the others as they went below for a sleep.

The wind picked up to 10 knots and *Antipodean* skimmed along with Grot not setting any particular course.

The yacht did not have any navigational lights and big freighters could not see her unless they had their radar switched on. Suddenly, in front heading towards them loomed another huge Russian tanker and before Grot realised it, *Antipodean* was within its shadow.

"Shit, I'm going to hit a big fuckin' tanker," he yelled below.

Peering through the hatch Roscoe and Sam went white with fear. As she was about to hit, the tanker's bowman pushed at the yacht with what appeared to be an exceptionally long boat hook.

Towering above them was a wall of steel and rusty rivets. On the fly bridge was the captain screaming and gesturing with his hands.

Down came the main, the jib and mizzen sails. The tanker gradually drew away leaving *Antipodean* bobbing around in its wake.

"You're sacked, you nearly got us fuckin' killed, Grot," said Captain Kaffir. "No more work on the steering wheel for you."

It was mid-June when *Antipodean* under full sail and making six knots sailed into Tunis and moored at the yacht club pier.

The next five days were spent emptying the bilges, waxing cracks on the inside of the hull, filling gaps that had appeared around the tiller stock, bailing water and repairing the shrouds with plastic hosing. *Antipodean* was also lifted out of the water for scrapping, anti-fouling and sealing the underside cracks.

Anti-fouling and scraping the hull in Tunisa

"Are you sure that these ragheads know what they're doing?" asked Roscoe.

"Well, they've got the mast out okay. That's a good start," replied Sam.

"Gee, that's not too bad," said Kaffir observing the hull. "There's a lot of stuff grown there. I'll get them to scrape it, dry the boat overnight and they can paint it in the morning. Meanwhile, I'll get the local engineer to make up a bracket for the rudder."

The next day the job was satisfactory completed.

"Here's your bill," one said. It was for £9.50.

"That's an extraordinary bloody good deal," said Kaffir handing over the cash.

Supplies were topped up, a crane dropped *Antipodean* back into the water and the mast was stepped, all without incident. They gathered on deck to survey the work of the last few days when without warning Grot vomited onto the side of the pier.

"Your food's bloody awful, Roscoe," he said.

"Yeah. How much have you had to drink? There's nothing wrong with my stew."

"I've been drinking for two days. It's not the piss. It's your cooking!"

"How come you always blame the food when you have a chunder?"

"Because my guts rumble."

"Yeah. Sure, sure."

They were on their way again. Progress was good. For the next 12 hours the boat averaged five knots. It was the longest period the genoa had been up. History had been made.

Then an easterly wind of around 35 knots came in bringing the sea with it. Water swept over the yacht for the next six hours. At 4.am, one of the seams on the main, ripped across the full width of the sail. It flapped wildly in the wind. Peter managed to get it down and crank up the motor. It was decided to ride out the bad weather.

Antipodean limped along until early afternoon while the crew dozed below. At 4.00pm, Kaffir, who was at the helm, called down to Grot, "Come up and tie down the loose foresail. The sea's swelling up to six feet."

Grot set about bringing down the jib. Suddenly without warning a wave struck, sending him sprawling through the rail which broke on impact into the sea. Under water he kicked himself off the hull, narrowly missing the prop. The impeller, trailing 50 feet behind the yacht, went spinning past. In desperation he lunged at it, but it disappeared in a blur. Surfacing, he could see *Antipodean* disappearing into the distance. His cries for help went unheeded in the wind.

On deck Kaffir continued issuing instructions and hearing no reply, turned to see Grot in the wake of the yacht.

"Man overboard," he yelled.

But with the noise of the motor no one below could hear him. Jumping through the cockpit, he roused the others. They all gathered on deck looking vainly out to sea.

"Shit, what are we going to do. I think he's done for. There will be an inquiry and a lot of questions asked," said Peter.

"Who's going to tell his parents?" asked Roscoe.

"I didn't know he had any relatives. I reckon it's your job as skipper," added Sam.

"We'll keep looking until we find his body and then head for the nearest port," gulped Kaffir, turning the boat around. Everyone went quiet as they scanned the ocean. Heads were down and there was emotion all round. In despair Kaffir turned to Peter.

"Pete, we'll winch you up the main. It's our only chance to spot him. Be bloody careful, 'cos the swell will really rock you about."

Peter was winched up the mast but with *Antipodean* rocking violently he could only make it to the cross trees. Holding on grimly with his arms wrapped around the mast and with the rigging spikes tearing at his arms, Peter peered all around him. There was silence. It seemed like an eternity.

Suddenly, Peter screamed, "There he is to starboard."

Grot was about 150 yards away floating motionlessly in the sea swell. It seemed an eternity before the boat drew alongside and with the engine turned off, he was hauled back on-board. Sam began CPR as Grot lay spread eagled on deck with a faint pulse. Sam kept resuscitating and after 15 minutes his groaning turned into intermittent breathing and then gave way to incoherent foul language. He was alive, there was no doubt about that.

It was a narrow escape and the second time he had been saved from drowning. Everyone was stunned by the experience. Not a word was uttered by anyone for the next hour or so. The shock of what had happened affected everyone.

It was decided to stop off at Pantelleria, a small island 62 miles southwest of Sicily and 45 miles east of the Tunisian coast. It was the ideal place to stop for a few days. The island endowed with a jagged coastline was lapped by clear blue seas that hid a wealth of varied marine life. The hot weather although constantly being tempered by ever-present strong sea winds, made it an ideal place to relax. Large bottles of beer cost 30 pence. The beach with its clear water was inviting. Hours were spent spear fishing but with little success.

They arranged for the main sail tear to be sewn back together by two old local Italian women. The boys hit the town each day going from bar to bar.

"Tomorrow is the island's festival day. I reckon we help celebrate that and then get cracking," suggested Peter.

The following day, most of the island's 1000 or so inhabitants crowded into the port eating and drinking from long trestle tables enjoying a typical Italian celebration. The crew were mostly drinking. It was late in the day when it was decided to leave. A large crowd gathered on the pier to watch their departure.

All went well until *Antipodean* motored just beyond the breakwater. A huge swell suddenly hit the boat lurching it sideways.

"Shit, the anchor's sliding across the deck. Grab it," yelled Sam.

"I can't. The chain and rope will rip my hands," replied Roscoe instantly.

"Who forgot to secure it after the boat overhaul in Tunis?" asked Roscoe as the heavy anchor, complete with its rope and chain, disappeared over the side into the harbour entrance.

"Turn the boat, Grot. I'll dive for it," said Peter, who still remained the fittest and most athletic of the crew.

Antipodean was turned and Peter started to duck dive searching fruitlessly. The swells increased in the wind. "It's too bloody deep, the anchor's gone," he reported.

"Let's keep going and head for Malta," said Kaffir, with one eye on the shore as the crowd looked on.

The main sail was raised, but as soon as it got to the cross-trees, it popped out of its track.

"We'll have to go back to port and sort all this out."

The crowd continued to look on as *Antipodean* attempted to lay anchor. But, with the main anchor lost, the small sand anchor was unable to stabilise the boat. *Antipodean* was bobbing around out of control. The crowd began yelling advice and waving their arms.

They began to cheer when an old unshaven, overweight character motored out to them and climbed aboard gesturing and speaking loudly in Italian.

"What's this cockroach want?" asked Grot. "We can't understand the prick."

"I think he wants to take us somewhere else," replied Kaffir.

Under motor and their new friend at the tiller, the yacht proceeded to a more sheltered bay crowded with local fishing boats. However, he didn't realise that *Antipodeans'* reverse was non-existent. Pulling sharply in vain on the gear stick, *Antipodean* just continued to plough forward ramming one of the fishing boats with the bowsprit.

Their new friend grimaced. The old Italian, muttering obscenities, finally secured *Antipodean* next to a fishing trawler and gratefully accepted a half drunken bottle of scotch for his trouble.

In the morning, they were awakened early by an Italian with a thick English accent.

"Hey. Have you people got any English tea? I'll swap some bottles of wine with you."

"Who are you?"

"I'm a Pantellerian who spent some time in England and boy, do I miss a cup of English tea."

"Let's do the right thing and give him our tea bags," said Roscoe. The crew searched the stores for a box, but to no avail.

"That bastard Kiwi Ted must have used them all in Gib," said Kaffir. "Sorry mate, but we don't have any. Can we have the bottles of wine anyway?"

"No!"

The next day, fresh supplies were purchased from the local market. In perfect sailing conditions with a 10-knot breeze and an even swell, the yacht sailed out of the bay for Malta, some 190 miles away. The sun beat down as she made good unhindered progress. The crew sunbathed nude on deck and Grot behaved himself.

A month had now passed since the final sea trial in Gibraltar. Confidence was growing by the day.

At 2.00am on 3rd July after 40 hours sailing, Malta came into view. Without incidence *Antipodean* moored at an ideal marina location in the Port of Valletta, a deep-water harbour extending about two miles inland.

Fees were exceptionally attractive. The first week was free and 7p each day thereafter. Nearby were excellent cheap restaurants, a laundry, ship chandlers and plenty of bars with comfortable outdoor seating shaded by high umbrellas.

That night the boys tucked into big steaks and then relaxed watching the semi-finals of the soccer World Cup, cheering West Germany into the final.

After asking around, a replacement main anchor was found in a ship's wrecker's yard. It was old and rusted but the rope and chain were in good condition.

"That will do us," said Kaffir, passing over £1.00.

"I only take lira."

"OK. We'll come back soon with the money. The anchor was taken away and no one returned.

In one of the bars they started talking to an Englishman called Jack who had just bought a 32 feet Dutch built yacht. Jack turned out to be a friendly sort of chap and after a while invited them to join him aboard for a few drinks with some of the locals.

"Let's show this Pommy bastard a thing or two," suggested Grot. "I'll organise the grog."

So with three bottles of gin, two of bourbon and champagne, two bottles of cheap local wine, three dozen tonic waters and two dozen ginger ales, but no food, the crew arrived. It was the mother of all parties. The Mersey sound of the 60s blared out across the harbour. The boys constantly harassed the Maltese girls with one thing in mind – to get into their pants. But being good catholic girls they were impossible to crack. All they got was a gigantic hangover.

After a couple of days of recovery, they set sail for the tiny island of Gozo and the other small islands in the Malta group. Spear fishing and chatting up the local girls, occupied most of the time. The soccer World Cup final came and went, but the local girls were keeping their panties on.

"What's that over there?" asked Peter one morning.

"It's a dog swimming across the bay," replied Grot.

"Let's take a look."

The two of them climbed in the tender and rowed across to the dog that was exhausted, barely able to paddle.

"It's an Alsatian and it looks like he's been in the water for hours. Here boy. Here boy," coaxed Peter. The dog just stared at them. There was obviously a language problem. Peter jumped in the water and swam beside it, but the dog began to snap and made numerous attempts to bite the Good Samaritan.

"He loves you," said Grot grinning. "We can't leave him here to drown though."

Pete moved in behind the dog and put his hands on the dog's neck and guided him slowly towards Grot. By now the dog was almost sinking. Peter gripped him under his forelegs and with Grot leaning over the tender, clasping the dog's rear; they tried to haul him aboard.

"Shit he's like a bag of cement. On the count of three, lift," said Peter. The tender which was dangerously rocking to and fro, almost capsized, but eventually the dog was hauled aboard. Exhausted they gathered their breath and looked at the dog that lay whimpering at their feet.

"What do we do with him now?" asked Peter.

"Get him ashore and find the owner," Grot replied. "There could be some free drinks in it for us." The tender made the slipway but before they could do anything the dog stood up, jumped off the boat and ran off.

"Grateful fuckin' dog."

"What did you expect," said Grot. "A blow job!"

The fact that *Antipodean* was still unregistered was playing on Kaffir's mind, "I'm going to see if I can register her with a bit of bullshit," he said.

Finding his way to the harbour office he was met with the usual reply.

"Sorry. If you don't live here or own a business, we can't do it."

"But we do live here."

"That's not what I've heard."

Meanwhile Sam began attracting a lot of attention with his easygoing nature, blond beard and blond afro hair. Lance, a local bar owner introduced him to the red light district. After one visit, Sam became the most sought-after man in town by the local prostitutes.

"These local girls are giving me the shits. They keep pestering me. They won't leave me alone. Let's get out of here," he said.

As they were finishing their farewell drinks, Lance introduced them to two English girls who had been hanging around the bar.

"This is Dianne and Heather. They're looking for a ride to Greece. That's where you guys are heading, right?"

"Yeah we are," said Grot, his eyes widening with anticipation. We're leaving later this afternoon. Do you want to come with us?"

"Yes, that would be nice," said Dianne without hesitation.

"Okay, but first I want to explain the rules we have on the boat," replied Grot without consulting the others.

"We sunbathe naked and expect you to do the same. Our sleeping quarters are cramped, so you will have to snuggle up with us during the voyage. I'm getting tired of Roscoe's cooking so it would be nice for a change. Do you still want to come with us?" The girls apprehensively slowly nodded their approval.

On board a modification was immediately undertaken inside the cabin. The rear section was converted into a double bed in anticipation of any activities that might occur.

So on a very hot and sunny afternoon on flat and glassy seas, the main and genoa were hoisted into a light south westerly. *Antipodean* sailed without incident out of the harbour, destination Greece.

Di and Heather were settling in nicely. On the first day, their backsides were bright red from the sun. The boys insisted they sit cross legged and play cards and scrabble on deck. Grot was having a ball, perving at every opportunity.

On the second day, it was getting too much for him and when Di said she was going below deck to read, Grot and Peter followed.

"I've got some shaving cream. Would you like us to shave under your arm pits?" asked Grot.

Hesitantly she agreed. With Peter holding her arm aloft, Grot went to work with the razor.

"Now the other one, please," he said.

"You're not a bad surgeon. I reckon you've missed your calling in life Grot," said Peter.

"There's more work to be done," was the reply.

Peter and Grot covered her body in the cream and began caressing and massaging her.

"That's nice," murmured Di.

"You've got a very bushy map of Tasmania. I've been worried about it. It's got to go," stated the Grot, authoritatively.

He began delicately shaving her pubic hair, methodically wiping the hair and cream away with his fingers which also did a bit of probing. It was all too much for Di. She spreadeagled her legs moaning and whispering, "Yes, yes."

Soon they all lay exhausted, but weren't finished yet. Putting more shaving cream over her breasts, Grot began flicking his flaccid penis at her nipples. It was a mini game of golf. Peter attacked the other. Shaving cream was merrily being flicked from her body onto the walls of the cabin. By this time, the giggling and noise attracted the others who crowded around offering advice.

"We've both got a hole in one," said Grot triumphantly. "It's the first British Open played at sea."

"Yeah, but we didn't win a car for the effort," said Peter.

The rest of the day passed without further incident until Sam began experimenting with the plastic sextant he had acquired while the boat was moored at Oliver's island.

"I reckon if we stay on this course we should pass the shoe of Italy," he said pointing into the distance. "Over there," he said turning, "is Greece."

"I can't see any land, Sammy," said Kaffir.

"Trust me. I'm getting better at this stuff. Keep on this course."

In the morning, land was sighted. "Is that Italy, Yugoslavia, Albania or Greece?" asked Kaffir peering at the school atlas.

"I think it's Greece."

"OK, let's go south a bit."

Antipodean continued this time under motor. She chugged along until mid-afternoon when off to port the islands of Peloponnese came into view.

The yacht entered the Messenian Gulf and the harbour of Kalamata, the second-largest city in southern Greece 147 miles south west of Athens. Its long beaches and easy accessibility by bus and train to other Greek cities and by ferry to places such as the Greek islands of Kythira and Crete made it a fortuitous stop over.

Antipodean laid anchor. Eventually, the quarantine officer came aboard. Formalities were completed and the yacht tied up. Everyone headed into town and found a bar to get their bearings.

"Don't you think you're drinking too much of that ouzo stuff, Di?" asked Sam after three rounds. "I'm on a mission to get pissed," she mumbled.

"I think she is feeling guilty about the other afternoon," said Grot. "I don't know why," he said, as Di promptly got up and stumbled out of the bar back to the boat.

The others stayed, drinking large quantities of retsina and ouzo mixed with coke. They wanted to test themselves as to how much they could drink of this new cheap booze. It was not a good experiment. The next day was very quiet indeed.

That night everyone discussed their next move. There were plenty of options. Side trips to the Greek Islands, stay where they were, head inland by bus and explore or target Athens collecting mail and catch up with others at the camping ground.

After much discussion Kaffir summed up, "Okay, it's agreed. Di, Heather, Roscoe and I will hitch-hike to Athens to the Poste Restante. "Sam, Peter and Grot – you stay here. Get pissed and look after the boat."

Turning to the girls he said, "Now we'll draw lots to see who travels with whom. We'll make it a race. The first to the corner of that big camping ground just outside Athens – the one that the Woodland Garden girls told me about," he said elaborating on the directions.

"I know it. Sounds good to me," replied Roscoe.

Basic belongings were squashed into a back pack and the challenge began in earnest at day break. Di and Kaffir were the first to leave choosing a minor route via Sparti and Argos, before linking with the main highway to Athens from Korinthos. Roscoe and Heather chose the main highway direct to Tripoli, Korinthos and Athens.

Di and Kaffir wandered out of town.

"Now, you stand here and put your thumb out. I'll lie on the ground and doze until you pull a lift," said Kaffir. "They are more likely to stop for a Sheila."

After a few hours, Di was complaining bitterly, "I'm sick of these big fat Greeks stopping and propositioning me," she said. "They think I'm one of those curb side prostitutes. It's your turn now."

Within the hour a truck driver stopped and after a chat in broken English, agreed to take them.

"You sit by the window and I'll sit in the middle."

"That's very considerate of you. That's a nice change, Kaffir, thanks."

They hadn't gone far when the driver insisted on stopping at a large roadside truck stop. The driver insisted they join him inside for a drink and a snack.

"Have a scotch and we'll take some beers for company," he said ordering an ouso for himself. Idle chit chat followed before they finally left.

During next 65 miles, he stopped at four roadside bars. Kaffir's head was beginning to spin. The hot sun reflecting off the windscreen did not help.

"I'm sick of drinking bad scotch and warm coke. I think this bloke's trying to get me pissed," he complained.

"Don't worry, Kaffir, I'm not drinking. Let's truck on and see what happens."

After about six hours and more stops at tiny villages among twisting narrow roads, the truck eventually headed towards a small cluster of houses on the outskirts of Athens.

"You meet my parents. You have a meal with me," he said. "Then we go night club together."

"Shit, this is good value," Kaffir muttered. "What a generous bastard!"

"I'm with you," said Di. "Let's do it."

After a huge meal consisting of homemade spanakopita followed by mousaka and finished off with big chunks of feta cheese, the three of them left for the night club life in central Athens. The truck driver certainly knew his way around. He was warmly welcomed in a dark and perfumed small night club, pumping out horrible loud Greek music sung in a high-pitched voice. Almost immediately the Greek truck driver asked Kaffir to dance with him.

"I suppose this is what Greek men do," Kaffir said to Di. "I hope you don't mind."

About half an hour and three dances later, their new friend started to cuddle Kaffir.

"Fuck. He's a bloody poofter. When he goes to the dunny, let's get the hell out of here."

When they left, Di couldn't stop laughing.

"What's so funny?"

"I knew all the time he was a pillow bitter. Actually, it's the first time I've felt safe for years!"

Asking directions and walking for about an hour, the two of them finally made their way to the camping ground arriving well after midnight. Stumbling around the huge camping ground, tripping over tent guide ropes and sleeping bags, the prospect of meeting Roscoe and Heather was unlikely. Kaffir began unrolling their sleeping bags intent on finding Roscoe in the morning.

Suddenly, someone grabbed his leg and bit him on his ankle. It was Roscoe. There were hand slaps all round. Everyone had arrived safe and sound.

Back in Kalamata, the others were having fun of their own. Grot would ask Sam to winch him up to the cross-trees where he would jump or dive into the water.

"I'm not sure if they think you are a daredevil or a bloody idiot," said Peter, eyeing a watching crowd on the wharf.

"Get me up again."

Grot finally decided to take a break and began eating water melon laced with gin. This deadly combination was not good for his health. He began doing somersaults off the deck into the harbour.

"Take it easy mate. Your audience has gone home."

"Just one more for the road!"

Taking a running jump he mistimed his landing and instead of the water his face hit the deck with a dull thud. Blood began gushing from above his left eye.

"Let me have a look at that. Christ, you need stitches. Your face is fucked," exclaimed Peter.

"That's sure a hellava gash," said Sam.

Grot went white in the face as blood began running down his chin dripping onto his chest.

"We'd better get a cab and get the poor bastard sorted," said Peter as they made their way ashore. Grot by now began shaking nervously with fear.

"Hospital, hospital," was all Sam could utter to the taxi driver.

The hospital was run by the Greek army and its patients were mostly tough ex-army personnel. And this new patient was a big strong Aussie! With the help of an interpreter Grot was escorted from the emergency ward into a small room. There was a knock on the door and a nurse carrying a clipboard and a needle entered.

"What's that needle for? I don't need a jab. I just want to go home," said Grot yelling with fear.

"I need to give you penicillin and do a blood test."

"I'm fine. I've had penicillin and I'm not allergic to anything, I swear."

"Okay, come with me."

About 10 minutes later, a doctor emerged laughing heartily.

"I went to give your big tough Aussie mate a local anaesthetic and guess what? He just fainted on me. He's out cold. I thought you guys were brave?"

"So did we," said Sam grinning. "He's as weak as piss."

For the next seven days, Grot was decidedly quiet as the three of them sought ways to relieve the boredom. The town was becoming quiet. Greece was at war with Turkey and the local men were being bussed to Athens to enlist. Time was spent playing pool and perving on the local talent. Acquaintances were made and quickly forgotten. The Greek girls were proving tricky to come across. Only Peter scored in this port and she was an American drunk on a night of drinking Tia Maria and milk.

The boys were relieved when the Athens foursome arrived back.

"Let's get trucking," suggested Peter, after stories had been swapped.

"Not before we make a new bowsprit," ordered Captain Kaffir. It was all hands on deck.

Because timber and bolts were difficult to obtain the job took two days but by that time, Di and Heather had thoroughly cleaned the inside of the boat. Everybody was ready for the next leg of the journey.

"I'm setting a course for the Greek Islands," announced Sam.

"Which one, Sammy?"

"Don't know. It will be a surprise."

Making seven knots into a 25-knot wind the yacht headed off into the direction of the Greek Islands. To the starboard side Crete could be seen in the distance. A big school of porpoises played around the yacht bobbing and diving under the hull. The sun was beaming down. This was more like it.

"We're a bit too far south I think, Sam," said Roscoe on the helm.

"OK, wheel her left. We should see some islands soon."

The detour south added five hours extra sailing. The wind dropped and so *Antipodean* continued under motor. Instead of sighting land mid-afternoon, it was midnight when the shape of a bay with some twinkling lights could be seen in the semi darkness.

"Let's go in here," said Kaffir.

"There might be rocks."

"I don't think so. It looks like some sort of embankment."

Antipodean motored towards shore. In the distance the headlights of a car loomed around a road which circled the bay. It got closer and closer and then zoomed past within 50 yards of them. "Shit. That was close. We nearly ran ashore and parked on the road," said Sam.

They had arrived at the port of Adamas inside a large bay within the small island of Milos considered the safest natural port in the Aegean Sea. After a comfortable nights rest, everyone was up early and a stern mooring was easily effected at the tiny boat wharf 100 yards from the nearest bar.

It was another long drinking session. Beer and ouzo was the combination for the day. The bar was packed with tourists wanting to get off the island. When the war with Turkey broke out, most of the ferries that linked the islands were commandeered by the Greek navy. People were stranded on the islands not knowing just when they would get off.

Tourists began begging the crew to take them to a different island. Peter used this desperation to his advantage and immediately fell in love with a Danish girl and disappeared back on board with her.

"I know what we should do. Why don't we select eight of the best chicks and take them off the island," suggested Grot.

"Great idea," replied Roscoe.

"Who wants to cruise with us to another island in the morning?" yelled Grot balancing on a plastic chair and addressing the bar.

"Put your hands up."

The bar was a buzz. The Grot and Roscoe began circulating, seeking out the best-looking talent. Grot kept a list of all the girls on a beer coaster. Soon he had about 15 names. Peering around the bar, he had forgotten who was who.

"It's time for elimination," he said, referring to his list.

He began to circulate again to re-acquaint himself. After an hour or two, he called for attention.

A hush fell over the bar.

"The following have been selected."

Struggling with the pronunciation of the mostly foreign names, Grot did a good job much to the amusement of the bar.

"Be at the dock, dressed in fuck all at 9.00am."

At 9.30am, *Antipodean* slipped away with their eight new passengers – destination the long and narrow island of Sikinos between Ios and Folegandros. With an area of 25 square miles and a population of some 200 inhabitants, it promised to be the ideal hideaway for all sorts of mischief. But, right from the start, *Antipodean* ran into a 25–30 knot head wind which gusted wildly. She was riding high and dipping quickly. It was not long before the all-female passenger list began being sick. The vomiting started within the hour. Heads were buried in all the buckets while others hung precariously over the side. Under motor, she was making under two knots progress. The three-hour trip was now approaching nine hours.

Then without warning the winds suddenly increased. First the boat's flag pole snapped and then the radar deflector broke away. Spray continually hung over the boat. Everyone was soaking wet. At 6.30pm, *Antipodean* eventually moored alongside the ferry wharf.

The next three days were relatively quiet. There was not much to do except try and screw the passengers or climb a precipice which rose some 330 yards above the sea in the centre of the island. What a view! The island was mostly stony, although one section was covered in olive trees. The whitewashed stone hamlets of Horio and Kastro, which were only a few hundred metres apart, offered nothing in entertainment. Di and Heather spent hours cleaning the boat. The bilges were pumped and cookie Roscoe purchased fresh supplies. Some of the female passengers visited for drinks on board. Life was boring.

What Di and Heather didn't know was that the crew would use the girls' cameras to take photos of a very inappropriate nature. In port, the girls unwittingly would send the film back to their parents in the UK for developing.

A meeting was called and Sam reminded everyone that the ultimate aim was to honour a previous arrangement made with Mike and his girlfriend Sue to meet in Ios, the party island of Greece in early August.

It was now 29 July 1974.

"We'll head off in the morning," ordered Captain Kaffir.

Despite problems with the starter motor, *Antipodean* was on her way at sunrise. With a consistent force six wind, she tacked under full sail towards Ios, halfway between the islands of Naxos and Santorini. From a distance they could see that their new destination was to be a very hilly island with cliffs down to the sea on most sides.

"It looks like hard work to get a drink here," observed Grot. Looking through a pair of binoculars purchased in a market in Dellys.

Antipodean entered from the north east into Ormos harbour and anchored.

Safely moored in the harbour of Ormos, Ios

From the anchorage, they could see a donkey path that weaved up a steep hill to Chora, the main village perched on a hill overlooking the bay. It would take 15 minutes to struggle up the single narrow trail littered with donkey poo. Apart from Chora, the major focus of activity were a handful of bars and the popular beach of Mylopotas where, after partying through the night, large numbers of backpackers would crawl into their sleeping bags and sleep. Surprise, surprise!

Sitting cross legged on the dock were Mike and Sue who had been a 'travelling love nest' throughout Europe. Needless to say, they were pleased to see *Antipodean* arrive on time. Hours were spent swapping stories and adventures and drinking plenty of ouzo and coke.

It was a drink-a-thon for seven days.

Returning by foot down, the steep decline after midnight became all too much for Sam's dodgy knees. One night, he just could not make it all the way down and instead sought refuge for the night, curling up on the steps of what he thought was the entrance to a small villa. In the morning, he awoke to find that in actual fact he had tossed and turned in front of a donkey pen and was covered in donkey shit. His blond hair had thick streaks of black poo running through it and he stank to high heaven.

"I see you've been sleeping with the local whore," said Grot as Sam staggered on board.

"Where I've been is with your ancestors," quipped Sam.

Life was becoming tedious. The local café owners were beginning to tire of the drunken crew. It all became too much for one, when one night Kaffir began leaping from table to table, sending glasses and bottles crashing to the floor.

"Stop it. Stop it," urged the owner, chasing Kaffir around the crowded café.

"Your food is crap and the beer is warm. Take this."

With that he dropped his shorts and rotating on a table, 'brown eyed' the bar. There was chaos. A Greek patron called Con called the police and Kaffir was arrested for obscene exposure.

After formalities at the station including a false name and providing the name of the boat moored beside *Antipodean* he returned to the bar. Con could see that Kaffir was not happy.

"I'm sorry. Let's be friends. I have a gift for you," he said, offering a bottle of Demestica retsina, some grapes and local cheese. Together they drank and ate until Kaffir eventually collapsed in the corner. The morning was not kind. He was sick and hibernated for the day.

The following morning, he awoke and went on deck, after the heat of the day had made it uncomfortable for him to sleep below. He was surprised to find Peter on the helm sailing happily along under a gentle breeze.

"Where are we heading, mate? I thought we were anchored in the bay last night.

"We were," said Peter. "I woke up to find us drifting around in the ocean no land in sight."

"Where are we going, mate?"

"Dunno, mate."

"Where are we, mate?

"Dunno, mate."

"Shit, we must have drifted in the night. That old rusted anchor did not hold. Oh well, maybe if we tack back in the direction of the wind we might find Ios.

So at 4.00pm, six hours later, the *Antipodean* sailed back into the bay that they had drifted out of the night before. This was much to the delight of the rest of the crew who had spent the night on the beach and were convinced their mates had done a runner.

Sam didn't know whether to be happy or sad at their arrival because he had organised for a day sail to Sikonos for a party of German girls. The girls were convinced the boat didn't exist and that Sam had other devious ideas.

As the days went on Grot was at his worst, abusing all and sundry and was arrested for exposing himself and being a public nuisance. His night in jail was followed by Kaffir, who made a second visit. Roscoe also ended up in the arms of the law for being drunk and disorderly.

By now, Di and Heather were tiring of the company and had a chat about their future.

"I'm getting sick and tired of these guys," said Di. "All they want from us is to clean their bloody boat."

"I agree. It's time we returned to Athens. I'm sick of seeing them strut around with no clothes on. Besides, Mum has complained about the photos' she's developed and is worried about me."

Kaffir was in his bunk dozing when the two girls poked their heads into the cabin, to bid him farewell.

"Don't shit me, women, just fuck off." So they did and were never to be seen again.

It was decided to head south towards Crete with Mike and Sue taking over the double mattress that had looked after Di and Heather so well. As soon as *Antipodean* was out of the sheltered harbour, trouble started almost immediately. A howling gale buffeted the boat and *Antipodean* was having trouble handling the combination of white water and strong gusting winds.

The main mast was bending and shaking out of control. The strain and pressure was immense. Suddenly, a loud crack could be heard from below deck.

"Christ, the main mast has split down the full length," yelled Peter. "I can see right through it. It's stuffed."

"Don't panic," said Kaffir, as *Antipodean* began to career out of control. We'll fill the cracks with tar and bind it when we get to port.

"The halyard for the jib has jammed. I can't get the sail down," called Roscoe, adding to the drama.

It was a matter now of survival.

"All hands on deck," yelled the Captain.

"Mike and Peter put out the sea anchor. We'll run with that," ordered Kaffir.

"Okay."

For the next 24 hours, *Antipodean* struggled to stabilise using the lightweight sea anchor which consisted of two plastic beer crates tied to a long length of rope. Sue was suffering with sea sickness and clearly frightened by the experience.

"That's it. I'm getting off at the next port," she told Mike. "You're bloody crazy being on this heap of rubbish."

The sea gradually began to calm and the wind dropped. No one knew where they were. With no main sail, headway was slow. The engine was groaning and puffing smoke.

"I see you haven't improved your navigational skills, Sammy," said Mike, watching Sam trying to interpret the school atlas map of Greece.

"There's an island over there," replied Sam pointing into the distance. "Let's head for that."

With the jib half way up and the mizzen out, a brisk wind sprung up and pushed the yacht along at break neck speed and then died when *Antipodean* turned into the lee of the island. With Grot on the tiller, he was taking no prisoners. He fired the motor to full speed and headed for the pier. But he had misjudged the speed and distance. *Antipodean* hit the wharf with a solid thud that split the bowsprit. But this rush of blood was quickly forgotten. Everyone was glad to be back on land. They were on the island of Santorini; a small circular volcanic island located about 125 miles southeast from the Greece mainland.

After almost two days of blustery unpredictable winds and heavy seas, the weary crew was relieved to be in touch with land again. To celebrate Cook Roscoe lost no time in lighting the stove, cooking up a wonderful brunch of omelettes and tomatoes on toast.

"You guys must be starving?" asked the cook as everyone tucked into their first meal for 24 hours.

"This is just heaven," said Mike.

Everyone's demeanor changed for the better. Work was being done to repair the main mast. It was a pretty crude job but appeared solid.

Sue said nothing. After the chatting subsided, she spoke for the first time.

"It's better I leave you guys here. I said you were all crazy and nothing is going to change my mind."

"Yeah," said Mike. "I'll look after Sue. There's more travelling to be done."

Surrounded on three sides of Santorini were 330-yard high steep cliffs sloping down to the surrounding Aegean Sea. On the fourth side was a deep lagoon making it a safe sheltered harbour. The capital Fira, clung to the top of the cliff looking down to the lagoon.

By now Grot was broke. His near drowning out of Tunis had clearly affected him mentally and physically. He became sullen and quiet. His drinking binges were almost non-stop.

"I'm a bit worried about you, Gary," Sam said, addressing him formally.

"Don't you think you should stay off the grog a bit?"

"I just feel I've had enough. I'm exhausted," replied Grot, "I think it's time to head back to Athens."

"I've had a great trip. Thanks guys. I'll head to Athens with Sam when he goes to collect the mail and then back to England," he said, choking back tears.

"We'll be sorry to lose your good manners," chipped Roscoe.

"You know what?" said Kaffir. "If you'd have died at sea, I was going to name my next dog 'Grotty'."

"I'll call mine 'Kaffir', but I'm not sure what will happen when I call it," Grot replied, cheering up.

The next two days were spent celebrating the eminent departure of Sue, Mike and the Grot. But to do so it took them an hour in the hot sun to climb the steep donkey track up to the many bars. It was tough work and worse coming down, especially full of retsina, ouzo and beer.

"I'm buggered. I'm booking a donkey from now on," exclaimed Mike.

"How much is it?"

"Twenty drachma."

"Sounds like the best idea since we've been here."

So donkeys were booked for each day. They would line their donkeys and race up the steep track. The competition kept them amused, as did the numerous donkey poo fights when they returned to *Antipodean*. It was two days of bedlam.

"You know what," said Mike on their last night. "I'm sorry to leave this island. The sunsets and views have been fantastic."

"Too many tourists and hills for me," replied Sue.

Sam and Grot left by ferry for Athens the next day. Mike and Sue followed a few days later.

"We'll find our way to Piraeus and hunt you down," was Mike's parting shot.

Antipodean left Santorini quietly and without incident until the cook went to open the pressure cooker for the first meal at sea. It was full of donkey shit which stank to high heaven. On top was a note, "See ya later, suckers," Grot had left his final stamp on the crew!

With Sam's improving navigational skills, *Antipodean* made it safely back to Ios. The general idea was to lay off the grog a bit and spend time doing repairs to the boat. But every effort to dry out was unsuccessful. Most days were spent in the sea playing water polo, drinking a gallon jar of gin and doing the odd runner from bars and cafes.

At the top of the hill was a very obliging bar which they adopted as their local. Once a week two bottles of duty free Johnny Walker Scotch would be loaded into a back pack and sold to the bar owner. In exchange, the crew made 300% profit and drank for free. The police also drank at the same bar appreciating the genuine scotch rather than the whiskey contained in huge wicker clad glass jars that were siphoned off into scotch bottles. It was obvious that the bar owner was paying off the police because the genuine scotch had no custom seals on the bottles. In real terms, everyone was happy!

One of the kiwis that had been hanging around the boat in Ios previously turned up again. He got talking to Kaffir while he was fixing a new flag pole

"Where are you boys off to?"

"This is our final trial run before we sail her to Australia," replied Kaffir.

"Sounds a great challenge."

"Come aboard."

Kaffir and the visitor chatted over a few beers. The relationship grew after a few days and it transpired that Kaffir's new friend had a mechanical background. Fully aware that *Antipodean's* motor could blow up at any time, Kaffir invited him to a meeting to discuss the possibility of him replacing Grot.

His name was Quinton Ryan, a Canterbury farmer from the rugged South Island of New Zealand. He had been working on oil rigs for a period in Western Australia and then decided to head for Greece for a holiday. Right now he was out of work. A big strong Kiwi with hands like saucepans, he loved the outdoors and fiddling with anything mechanical.

"I think Quinton will fit in pretty well," Kaffir told the others. "His mechanical skills will be invaluable especially as the bloody motor is always playing up. Let's make him a paid up shareholder in the boat in exchange for his skills."

The others nodded in agreement.

'I'm not sure about his name though," said Peter. "It sounds a bit poofterish."

"We'll call him 'Anchor' after the one we lost in Pantellaria," said Kaffir.

Anchor fitted in well. On the first night as an official crew member, he was on his hands and knees crawling under the tables in the café biting the ankles of all the girls he came across. Roscoe joined in the fun eating and licking a plate of spaghetti on his hands and knees in the main square and barking like a dog.

Boredom was now the main problem. Nights were spent going from bar to bar, chatting up girls of every size and nationality. During the day, they would sleep or doze in recovery mode.

Eventually, Sam returned with the mail and was introduced to the new crew member. To celebrate everyone being together, it was agreed *Antipodean* should host a sangria party on board. The shopping list read like this:

2½ Tia Maria£ 2.50 3 Brandy 1.50
2 Vodka 4.50
20 Demestica Wine 11.00
24 Ginger Ale 1.50
24 Lemonade 1.50
1 Vermouth Gift
1 Rubbish Bin, plastic inner 2.00
Total £ 24.50

On Saturday morning Roscoe put on the Captain's hat.

He began pouring the ingredients into the bin, stirring as he did so. When all the liquid was poured, he again stirred vigorously with a broad smile on his face.

"This will shake up our guests," he said.

Word on the island spread fast and at noon, the party began. Within two hours more than 40 guests were crammed on board and the party was in full swing. By five o'clock almost everyone was drunk. Girls were tossed overboard, others lay flaked on the deck and one was carried off the boat and dumped on the pathway.

Those able to stand hit the disco until three in the morning. The crew's reputation on the island was becoming legendry. It also came to the notice of the police who would call by regularly asking them to leave the island.

The usual excuse of, "the motor won't work, we're awaiting repairs," was beginning to wear thin.

The crew's regular bar hunting and the sangria party improved their sex life out of sight. All managed to fall in love and get rid of topped up bags. Kaffir was in love.

He had fallen for a short, fair haired, rather plumpish American girl whom he originally referred to as just another 'Septic Tank'. But, it is amazing what a kiss and a cuddle will do to a man on a mission.

After two days of going missing with his new girlfriend nick named 'Sep', Kaffir eventually turned up with a broad grin on his face.

Roscoe admonished him. "We said no one was to fall in love. The deal was to get your end away and move on."

"Relax, relax. She's off to Athens in the morning and thinks I'm going to follow her back to the US."

"That's okay then."

In the morning, Kaffir was busily cuddling Sep on the pier waiting for the transit boat to take her out to the inter-island ferry. Anchor wandered by.

"Hey Anchor, why don't you come out with us to say good bye?"

"Yeah, okay."

Once aboard the inter-island ferry, Sep began waving from the deck.

"Let's give her a typical Kiwi farewell," suggested Anchor. Together they clambered onto the roof of the transit boat, braced their legs and wobbling around performed a very poor rendition of the haka. The final leap in the air was spectacular but disastrous. As they landed on the cabin roof it completely caved in, dumping them both on top of the startled crew member steering towards shore.

"Shit, we're in trouble now," said Anchor noting that the transit officer was already on the radio phone back to shore.

"You're right. Look over there. The police are waiting for us," said Kaffir as the boat neared the wharf.

"We'll have to run for it."

The two of them separated and ran off in different directions. Police were everywhere. Whistles and sirens were blaring out. It was as if the whole island's police force were waiting for this moment.

Kaffir, who was very unfit, was struggling as a posse of police closed in on him. Panting and gasping for breath he was caught, arrested, and frog marched along the foreshore.

"You're going to be deported off this island. We don't want you here," he was told at the station.

"I need an interpreter," said Kaffir stalling for time.

"Don't be foolish. You can understand us," the officer replied.

"I promise to be a good boy and leave as soon as the motor is fixed," said Kaffir. "And I'll pay for the damage," knowing he had no intension to do so.

"I want you to report to the ferry office first thing in the morning and make arrangements to pay the damage. The next time you're in trouble, you're in the cells and will be escorted back to Athens airport and then deported to wherever you came from," was the reply.

Sheepishly, he returned to the boat as the rest of the crew were celebrating Anchor's brush with the law.

"You need to work on your leg speed," said Anchor. Everyone roared with laughter.

From that moment on, the police would come down to the pier every day and shout, "Today, you go."

They also continually harassed Kaffir about paying the damage bill.

"They haven't got all the costs together yet," Kaffir would say each time.

This really annoyed the Police.

"Your motor must be fixed by now."

"No, we have a part coming tomorrow."

The police presence was now wearing thin with the local bar owners who began to side with the crew. They would come out and gesture with their hands, speaking loudly in Greek. The police would shrug their shoulders and wander off.

Opposite their mooring was a small café run by an old Greek woman. She adopted them and would always yell at the police when they were hounding the crew. To repay her they always had an early morning drink in her café.

"I'm not giving you any beer until you've had breakfast," she would say.

It was time to leave Ios. The good times on the island were well and truly over.

Monday, 2 September 1974, everyone woke up early in preparation to depart destination Sikinos.

Sam looking at the atlas was excited and emerging on deck pointing vaguely in a westerly direction towards the horizon.

"That's the course," he said. "Cast off."

Antipodean slipped away but emerging out of the lee of the bay she was hit with a strong wind.

"Christ, what's going on? The mast's wobbling about," yelled Roscoe. "I hope the tar and binding will withstand the strain. We don't want the split to get worse."

148

"I don't think it will get worse," said Kaffir gazing skyward. "As soon as we hit Sikinos and find a bay, we'll make more permanent repairs."

Antipodean limped into the small bay called Malta on the tip of Sikinos, about 4 miles from the main island village of Chora. High up on a cliff was a blasting gang. Rocks were cascading down the slope into the tiny bay.

"Plenty of action here," said Anchor motoring closer to shore. "There seems to be a very small rundown café over there," he said pointing to the far end of the bay. "Let's go and take a look."

The owner got a shock when they entered. "We'll have five bottles of beer please," asked Peter politely.

"Sorry, I only have a keg of ouzo."

"We'll try that then."

Proudly the café owner tapped off five large glasses. They all raised them for a toast.

"To our trip across the Pacific!" was the chorus, glasses raised.

Clink! As one they had their first gulp.

"Ahh shit. This is unpalatable," choked Anchor eyeing the sludge in his glass and then slinging the rest of the deep yellow coloured liquid onto the concrete floor.

"Hey, don't do that. The villagers like this. Just because you tourists are not trained on homemade ouzo there is no need to make a mockery of our traditional drink."

"Yeah, you people just don't appreciate good quality grog," answered Anchor.

"I suggest you go up that track then," he replied, pointing to the bottom of the hill. "There's a small village there. That's where you can find beer."

An hour or so later threading up the narrow winding donkey track and sweating profusely, they stumbled onto a small cluster of houses and a single café. A faded umbrella hung over a stained plastic table with four chairs which protruded out into a tiny square. There was no one in sight. Plonking themselves down, they waited for service. The sun was beating down and after 10 minutes, Sam sauntered inside.

"Is anyone there?" There was no response. "Okay, then I'll help myself," he said to no one in particular.

With that the boys helped themselves to a huge ice box stacked with beer. Within two hours it was cleaned out.

"What do we do now?" asked Roscoe. "I don't think it's fair we just piss off without paying."

"It hasn't stopped you before," answered Anchor.

"Yeah, but these guys make fuck all money and are probably slaving away somewhere in the fields."

"Yeah, but we have fuck all money as well," said Sam.

"Let's leave a message saying we are down in the bay and if he wants to be paid, he should front down and see us."

"Good idea! Write it in scrawly long hand English. That way, he won't understand the message."

They trooped back to the boat. The next day with no grog within miles they set about making repairs without distraction. Anchor did some much needed wire splicing; Kaffir and Peter fixed new stays to support the main mast and spent hours fibreglassing the split. Sam, some needlework to mend a small rip in the jib and Roscoe spliced the anchor warp where a fishing boat had frayed it.

With everything ship shape in the morning, it was decided to make the short journey along the south eastern coast to the main port, identified by Sam as Alopronia. The sail of 2 and a half miles from Chora was uneventful but delayed by the lack of wind leaving them becalmed. Eventually mooring at midday, it was time to investigate the row of tavernas which were at either end of the small fishing village.

There was excitement in town. In the bars all the talk was about the forthcoming marriage of an American jet setter. Big luxury cruisers and boats were crowding into the port making *Antipodean* the preverbal 'ugly duckling'. Otherwise the place had a bit of class about it.

The boys went looking for action but were snubbed by all and sundry. Security was tight and they were sent away from the only bars worth drinking at.

It was now a week since leaving Ios. It was agreed that plans should be made to make the port of Pireaus, gateway to Athens 100 miles away on the Greek mainland.

In preparation, Roscoe tended to the remaining repairs, fixing hoses around the new shrouds and helping Peter with the on-going job of re-fibre glassing the mast.

After a night of violent thunder and lightning, lashed with southerly winds, the morning brought relative calm. *Antipodean* headed off into variable patches of wind ranging from no wind to strong gusts of up to 30 knots. The inconsistent conditions and rough seas played havoc with their progress.

"Shit, this is a worry. We're going nowhere. Probably going backwards," announced Captain Kaffir.

"I reckon we're only about 15 miles from Sikinos. The jib and mizzen are both stuffed and we can't tack in these conditions. Sam, look for shelter and let's lay anchor for the night."

Heading northward, Sam located a very small island he nominated as Poliegos. It looked uninhabited with just rocks and parched barren landscape visible along its short coast line, but it did offer shelter from the 30 knot winds which continued for the next two days. The time was spent sewing the sails, spear fishing and diving from the bow into the clear Aegean Sea.

Food was getting low. Four packets of soup, a dozen potatoes, half a pound of rice, two tins of sardines, spaghetti and chocolate powder was all that was left on board.

"We need more food. Like fresh fish. It's time for a spear fishing contest," suggested Peter. "Each team of two has five minutes in the sea and then we'll assess the catch. The winner will be based on the size of anything edible."

Lots were drawn. Kaffir and Roscoe were first off returning with a reasonable size mullet and a handful of sea urchin spines.

"That's a pretty lousy effort," said Peter, noticing Kaffir shaking his wrist. "What's with the hand?"

"Listen, I did spear an octopus but when I was trying to pull it out of a rock crevice, I put my hand on the rock for support. Instead of support I got a hand full of sea urchin spines in my hand. Shit it hurt. So I left the octopus there and now I'm in bloody agony," he said wringing his hand.

Sam and Peter didn't fare much better with one very tiny octopus for five minutes work. Everyone sat on the deck in silence which was eventually broken by Kaffir.

"I've been watching an old Greek guy walking along the beach at night with his goats. Why don't we lay in wait and spear one?" suggested Kaffir, grinning from ear to ear. With food of little substance on board, this sounded like a great idea.

"Here's the plan. Peter, you and Roscoe take the spear gun and hide behind those rocks over there and wait until the last goat is about to pass. We'll wait here and keep watch. If we signal by waving our arms abort the operation. No signal then fire. Make sure the spear sticks."

At dusk, Peter and Roscoe took up their positions and on schedule, the goats with bells around their necks, ringing in the still night air came into view.

"Are you sure the Greek guy is carrying a stick?" asked Sam squinting.

"Shit, I think it's a bloody shot gun," replied Anchor.

By now the line of goats were almost parallel with Peter who was poised ready to fire the spear gun.

"If he hits that bloody goat there'll be a hell of a racket and the Greek guy will probably go berserk and someone will be shot," panicked Kaffir.

The three of them stood on the deck and began waving their arms vigorously.

Glancing towards the boat, Roscoe nudged Peter. "The boys are all waving their arms, that's the signal to abort."

A little while later, the two of them waded out to the yacht carrying bunches of grapes and a large supply of vegetables wrapped in their tee shirts.

"What's that you've got?"

"We didn't spear his goat so we raided his garden instead!"

It was Thursday, 12 September 1974, when *Antipodean* was guided to a spare berth in the marina of Mikrolimano, the smallest of the three ports in Piraeus. It was a beautiful little harbour, crowded with a mixture of fishing boats, small boats and luxury yachts. Their berth was just a gentle stroll to their new home, 'The Plum Pudding'.

'The Plumb Pudding' was, if not by name, a typical Greek tavern. There was freshly made daily bread, plenty of lamb and fish options, traditional Greek salads, soups and various appetisers. Tzatziki. Tirokafteri, spanakopita and dolmades dominated the menu chalked in Greek on the blackboard outside. It also had ice cold beer and local ouzo and retsina bottles which lined the shelving behind the bar.

The 17 days in Piraeus were spent acquiring equipment, overhauling the motor and plenty of drinking, mischief and scheming at 'The Plum Pudding'.

The crew were also re-acquainted with Mike and Sue who true to their word had tracked them down. After the usual embraces and hugs, everyone settled down to reminisce on their adventures.

"I remember that day on Easter Thursday last year, how you and Ted 'The Dart' showed up in Gib out of the blue with three new sails for the yacht. That was good news in a hurry because what we had, was stuffed," said Kaffir.

"Yeah, it sure made a difference. By the way, you bastards never paid us for those sails," said Mike.

"Just put it on the tab," replied Sam. "So what did you guys do next?"

'The Dart' and I went back to London and worked until June. Then Sue and I flew out to Cairo and travelled around Egypt, Cyprus and Israel. Bloody pollution in Cairo was unbearable. After that we flew to Greece and caught the ferry out to Ios, expecting to see you, whenever. We arrived in fact, just one day before we had arranged to meet you guys. Sue and I had to sleep on the beach for only one night, before spotting you all on the wharf the next day.

"It was a real shock. I kept saying to Sue, they will never arrive on time. We'll be waiting the whole summer for them. By the way Sam, thanks for letting us use your wank tank."

"Yeah, it was my bed for 18 months, but I reckon Sue wouldn't have been real happy about sleeping there."

"It had just a tiny bit of privacy, thank god," sighed Mike. "Do you remember the time we sailed over to a small island to give Suzie a taste of real sailing? We came back at night under sail. The wind had dropped and the motor wasn't working so the only way to make any progress was to throw a bucket over the side and drag it through the water. When we approached the berth, I think you and Peter put on flippers and holding on to the bowsprit tried to physically turn the boat around."

"Christ it was funny. We laughed our heads off. Remember how we successfully backed in twice under full sail into those 'stern to' moorings. I think we had read how to do it in a magazine. We just came in and swung around, dropped the main and the jib, backed the mizzen out and she just came straight back in," said Peter.

"That's right. We were right next to a big luxury motor cruiser and scared the living shits out of them. They were all very impressed though. I don't think they had ever seen anyone back into a bloody slot under full sail like that before," said Mike.

And so the stories went on becoming more exaggerated, as the hours passed.

There was never a dull moment in Piraeus.

Roscoe went AWOL into Athens and shacked up in town with one of the passengers who he bumped into in the street and was so very kind to him on Sikinos.

Peter celebrated his birthday by falling in love while Sam went off looking for a sewing machine.

"I'm sick of all this hand mending of the sails," he said poking around in a market. Eventually, he found an old hand sewing machine. It had a little hand wheel and was a bargain for £5. Lugging it back on board he explained, "If you thread the sails through here, turn up the seams, wind the hand drive, then vroom, vroom, pull the sail through and the job will be done."

"Yeah, yeah, sure, sure."

The bargain of the year was never used successfully. It jammed the first time and attempting to wrench it free, Sam broke the needle.

"Why didn't you buy some spare needles as well?" asked Anchor.

"What do you expect for 5 quid? The latest model Singer sewing machine with oil can and a box of diamond needles?" was Sam's reply.

"Reminds me of Kiwi Ted's cheap dinghy at Oliver's Island," muttered Kaffir.

It was imperative that the motor be overhauled so many hours were spent asking around for a competent marine engineer. The port was full of so-called experts all to make a quick and easy drachma. The locals were well aware of the motto, 'they're here today and gone tomorrow'.

Eventually, an elderly Greek man operating out of a ramshackle office on the quay agreed to do an overhaul. The motor was taken out and then three days later replaced for £120.

This was money not well spent and its failure at the most critical time, contributed to the drama which was to unfold.

During the Pireaus stop over the local Greek community gradually embraced the sailors. Anything asked for was given. Anchors, ropes, machine bolts, cleats, deck plates, a nut wrench, hose connectors, even buoyancy vests.

Kaffir and Anchor also underwent their own sorties. One night they borrowed a dinghy off the jetty and rowed towards a sloop about 100 yards off shore. In the still of the night, they slipped alongside as the occupants slept.

"Anchor, you lie on the deck and be ready to catch the halyard when I release it off the mast," ordered Kaffir. Delicately, Kaffir pulled the halyard down and let it flop onto Anchor's chest. Smothered in the sail he lay motionless and on Kaffir's signal together they bundled it into the dinghy and rowed silently away.

"We should set up a marine used equipment shop and sell stuff back to the rightful owners," suggested Anchor. They both laughed heartily.

The Plum Pudding was a meeting place for all sorts of odd characters. One was the caretaker for an 80ft old galleon moored about 50 yards away from *Antipodean*. It had been used for the movie 'The Three Musketeers'. One night, drinking with the caretaker they learnt it had been partially gutted inside, but it still had its echo sounder and ship to shore radio.

"Now that will be an ideal acquisition to get us across the Pacific," whispered Kaffir out of ear shot.

"Yeah, let's knock it off."

"Okay. Sam, you and Mike get this guy pissed and Anchor and I will grab someone's dinghy and pay a visit to the galleon."

The commandeering of one of many tenders up on the wharf was easy. They lowered it into the water and pushed off and settled between the galleon and the wharf.

Kaffir clambered on board and dropped through a hatchway but halfway through the process of disconnecting the radio, he heard Anchor screaming at the top of his voice.

"Kaffir, Kaffir, can you hear me? The wind is forcing the ship against the dinghy which has sprung a leak. Shit, I'm being crushed against the wharf."

155

Using his arms and legs Anchor braced and tried desperately to fend off the galleon but within minutes, the dinghy began taking water at a fast rate. The weight of the heavy galleon battered and then crushed the dinghy against the quay wall.

Panicking, Anchor stood and wobbling about managed to grab a mooring bollard and with difficulty, hauled himself up onto the wharf. Extending a hand, Kaffir followed. The dinghy was smashed against the sea wall, broke up and sank with the ship's radio meeting a watery death.

"You know what? That dinghy had its bung removed to drain the water out. That's why it was on the wharf. Thank goodness we weren't 100 yards away," said Kaffir.

Gordon was another character they got to know at The Plum Pudding. Two years previously he, his brother and some mates had bought a MTV World War 2 motor torpedo boat.

To finance their purchase they advertised in the 'London Times' travel classifieds the headline 'Trip of a lifetime to Athens on a luxury launch'. About 30 punters paid up for the privilege and the money was then used to pay for the aging boat.

But the voyage down to Greece was a disaster. Sleeping accommodation consisted of hammocks strung up around the boat, food was in short supply, the boat was unseaworthy and continuously took in water and everyone was seasick. By the time they reached Gibraltar everyone bar two, deserted the boat never to return. The old ex-torpedo boat continued on its way, but just outside Pireaus harbour it ran aground on the rocks. After much conflict with the local harbour master, it was salvaged and towed into Athens with a writ slammed on Gordon, until the salvage fees and a hefty fine were paid.

Gordon and his brother did a runner and then waited 18 months before returning. Gordon's brother had a meeting with the harbour master and claimed that the boat was actually his.

"I haven't seen my brother for years and I'm looking for him too. He stole my boat. He's a crook." The salvage money was accepted and the two of them got out of Athens as quickly as they could and sailed the leaking boat to Malta where they moored in Valletta's Grand Harbour beside the pier.

While relaxing in the marina café having a couple of well-earned beers they saw a fire engine go past with its siren blaring. What they didn't realise was that their torpedo boat had taken in so much water it had partially sunk in the harbour and the fire engine had been summoned to pump the boat out. To avoid more salvage fees, they left Malta immediately. Nothing more was ever heard of the old World War 2 torpedo boat!

Another regular at The Plum Pudding was an American sailor, called Duane. He was in his mid-60s and drank only cheap rum – vast quantities of it. The boys loved his company.

"I've just taken possession of a yacht which I commissioned to break the cross Atlantic speed record," he told the boys. "Problem is, I can't sail it myself."

"Why's that?"

"It's a 90 footer with two 50 foot outriggers on either side. She sits high in the water with huge sails and no winches. Everything must be done by hand. Would you like to come out with me and have a sail?"

"You bet," Sam responded. "We've never been on a 90 foot outrigger."

A few days later, everyone met up with Duane and went aboard.

"This is a heap of old rubbish," Sam said surveying the deck. "There are too many pulleys and there's rope all over the place. Christ knows what belongs to what. Everything is cheap. The ropes, the sails, the lot," he said.

Safely out to sea they hoisted the sails. It was tough work – everyone having to identify then pull on the combination of ropes at the same time. It was back breaking stuff but in the light breeze the huge yacht moved swiftly over the water.

"This is bloody fantastic," said Sam. "Shit, she can move."

It was plenty of fun but returning to port the wind lifted to around 20 knots and the yacht suddenly took off, virtually out of control.

"All hands on deck," yelled Peter. "Get the main down."

All on board began pulling at the ropes. The pulleys croaked and groaned and the ropes became tangled. The pressure of the wind against the sails had everyone careering across the deck under the enormous strain to pull the spreaders in.

The mizzen mast crashed onto the deck and the cross-trees fell out. The badly designed boat was in serious trouble. Then the rope cleats on deck snapped under the pressure and broke away. But worse was to yet to come.

"Duane's crook. I think he's had a heart attack," yelled Sam.

"Oh shit. The poor old prick?"

"Don't panic. Do CPR Sam and I'll see if I can get her back to port. You boys just concentrate on getting the sails down anyway you can."

After another 20 minutes, the sails were all down but the deck was just one big mess with everything in a big tangle. Everyone was exhausted. Sam was relieved on CPR duties and soon Duane just lay groaning on deck.

"Use the radio and call for help. We've got to get Duane off the boat," said Sam.

"I can't figure out how to work this bloody radio. It's really old and the frequencies aren't set," said Kaffir.

"Let's just get her to shore and I'll go for help," offered Anchor.

Eventually the huge yacht was safely moored alongside the wharf, an ambulance called and Duane was rushed to hospital. The boys adjourned to The Plum Pudding.

"Shit, that was close. I reckon that yacht's stuffed," Sam said.

"It sure is. I hope Duane's not. I feel sorry for him," responded Kaffir.

The next day everyone crowded around Duane's hospital bed. He was a forlorn man.

"What are you going to do now, mate?"

"I think my sailing days are over," he said wiping away a tear. And so they were.

Financing the trip for the most part had been relatively easy. Whisky cost 89p a bottle in England and could easily be resold along the Mediterranean coast for twice the price. In particular, Johnny Walker Scotch and Marlboro cigarettes were the most in demand. The £200 worth of scotch and cigarettes purchased in London prior to departure were sold along the way to grateful bar owners making up to 300% profit for the crew.

Gibraltar and Malta were the two ports which allowed unlimited provisions unlike the 90-day allowance in England. The profits from the initial purchase provided a kitty to buy £300 worth of scotch and cigarettes in Gibraltar and later Malta. The bonded goods were put into a locked cupboard by customs with a customs seal.

The idea was that you couldn't go back into port and sell them at a profit to local bar owners. This didn't worry our crew who constantly broke the seal for on board consumption, buy more and re-sealed the cupboard themselves. This scenario was repeated time and time again in Gibraltar and Malta. Nobody really knew where the customs paper trail on all the transactions were but the profits were high and well worth the risk.

Supplies ready to be loaded on board.

At a team meeting on Monday 30 September 1974, it was decided to leave Pireaus at day break the following day and head for the Italian coast. Roscoe signed on again and with Sam and Peter, the trio headed for the Plum Pudding for farewell drinks with Mike and Sue, the travelling love nest. Kaffir and Anchor borrowed another dinghy and undertook a final sortie around the marina and collected a modest amount of equipment lying around on the deck of other boats.

So the following morning with no wind, *Antipodean* under motor headed for the famous Corinth Canal which separated the Peloponnese from mainland Greece. It provided a maritime short cut between the Gulf of Corinth and the Saronic Gulf and traced a straight line across the isthmus – the narrow neck of land joining the Peloponnese to mainland Greece.

Before the Corinth Canal was constructed in 1882, ships had to travel around the Peloponnese which added proximately 185 nautical miles and several days more travel to their journey time. The Canal was nearly two and a half miles long, 36 feet deep and 82 feet wide at water level. The walls rose to more than 80 yards at the highest point.

"Hell, this is awesome," said Anchor as the canal came into view.

Finally arriving at 7.00am, it was discovered that the canal did not open for several hours so the downtime was put to good use checking and re-storing the vast array of newly acquired equipment that had accumulated in Athens. Anchor began tinkering with the motor.

"I don't like the sound of the engine Kaffir," he said.

"Well, you had it repaired, remember? Keep an eye on it."

"I'll have another look at it when we make Patras," replied Anchor, "but it's really on its last legs I reckon."

Once through the canal a big ship loomed up behind them. "Shit, this bloke's chasing us down," yelled Peter to the others.

"Open up the throttle, Anchor."

The motor would not co-operate. Black smoke poured out of the engine and it began to knock. *Antipodean* sputtered on leaving a cloud of acrid black smoke and the chasing ship in its wake. Eventually, she laid anchor in the Bay of Patras just as the motor completely seized.

Located in western Greece, 135 miles west of Athens, the port of Patras was the main gateway to Greece from Italy and Western Europe. The Ionian Islands and Corfu were just a short ferry ride away and the south coast of Italy was well within an easy sail.

"So much for the £120 we forked out in Athens to have it overhauled," murmured Roscoe.

"Let's sail in, get a berth and maybe the mechanics are better here than those pricks on the marina at Pireaus, suggested Anchor.

With the help of the water police, a berth was provided in the merchant harbour just as darkness fell. Everyone headed off to the nearest bar to relax, leaving Anchor to ponder his next move to repair the old taxi motor.

He wasted no time in locating a company whose sign simply said 'We fix motors, guaranteed'.

When morning broke, an English speaking Greek with his mechanics were waiting dockside.

"Engine no go. You fix or no pay," said Anchor in broken English.

The three of them spent an hour talking and fiddling with the engine to no avail. The oil pump began to work but oil was not getting through to the gauge. The motor continued to make a loud screaming noise and pour smoke.

"Piss off. You've made it worse," Anchor said, waving them away.

"Look boys, I think the motor will move us along, but I don't know how fast or for how long," Anchor explained. "I suggest we crank it up and only use it getting in and out of port."

"OK, that sounds sensible," replied Kaffir. "It reminds me. I've been thinking for a change. Wouldn't it be great to do some night sailing?" he said.

"Yeah but we need a powerful spotlight – preferably two," replied Roscoe.

"Umm. What's that over there?"

"It's a customs compound," answered Roscoe.

"Exactly! Check out those heavy duty vehicles inside."

"I see what you mean."

Bolted to the roof of each was a sturdy looking spotlight.

"Leave this to me. You guys are on guard duty. Whistle if the police come." It took only a few minutes for Kaffir to slide under the gate, climb on top of the bonnet and begin unbolting one of the lights.

Just as Roscoe whistled a voice rang out.

"Put now it back now!" it said in broken English.

It was a policeman doing his security round.

"You come with me. You under arrest. Give me your wrist and slip into this."

With one wrist hand-cuffed, Kaffir was made to carry the bulky heavy spotlight along the merchant harbour waterfront and was then escorted up the main street.

The locals looked on and watched Kaffir with interest. It was all very embarrassing. At the police station, an interpreter was organised and Kaffir began explaining to the four duty police who were sitting opposite him why he had taken the light.

"Look, in New Zealand there are a lot of car compounds like yours and anyone is welcome to go in and help themselves to anything they like. I thought you had the same sort of compounds here."

The police looked at each other gesturing and speaking loudly in Greek over each other.

"I think they don't believe you," the interpreter told Kaffir. "They're going to get a senior officer to make a decision on how long you will stay in jail."

"Oh, shit."

When the senior officer arrived he asked Kaffir through the interpreter an extraordinary question.

"Have you read a book called 'Gulliver's Travels'?"

What on odd thing to ask, thought Kaffir.

"Why does he want to know?" he asked the interpreter.

The interpreter explained that the officer was halfway through the book when he had lost it and wanted to know what had happened.

"Do you remember where you up to?" asked Kaffir.

The officer explained as the other police looked on. Without hesitation Kaffir made up the rest of the book even though he had never read it. With the interpreter relating Kaffir's words carefully, the others also showed interest in the story that never was. The process took more than an hour as Kaffir got bolder and bolder and exaggerated any plot that came to mind.

The officer was impressed and obviously relieved that now he knew the end of the story.

"You come with me!" he said.

With that Kaffir was frog marched back to the compound and as the five police watched made to bolt the spotlight back on the truck. Then they took him to *Antipodean*.

"You leave – now!"

It was Saturday 6 October, *Antipodean,* under sail headed into a big estuary outside the bay. About 30 miles in the distance there was a lighthouse with its light flashing. "I'm off watch now – Peter, just head for the lighthouse." Kaffir said retiring to his bunk.

The only sounds that could be heard were the wind and the water lapping gently at *Antipodean*. Then in the early hours, everyone was awakened by a jolt and the sound of the boat groaning and creaking. She began to list. There was no sound of water lapping the yacht.

"What the fuck's happened?"

"We've run aground," replied Peter.

"Where's the lighthouse?"

"Up there! Above us," he said pointing skywards.

The lighthouse loomed over them, its base about 50 yards away. The yacht was well and truly stuck in mud and partly stuck in the silt that covered the concrete of the lighthouse foundation.

"You bloody idiot! Shit. How the fuck did this happened?"

"I nodded off," Peter, sheepishly replied.

"Okay, let's not worry about that now. We'll draw straws and the two losers will have to swim out in the freezing water with the heavy anchor and drop it out as far as possible," ordered Captain Kaffir.

The drawing of lots was not what Anchor and Sam wanted. After some discussion a rope was attached to the big old fisherman's anchor and was looped around Anchor's chest. With the aid of flippers, the two of them swam out to sea as far as the chain and rope would allow. Exhausted, they dropped it.

Returning to the lighthouse, they joined Kaffir standing in the mud and on the slippery concrete. The three of them began to push the bow sideways, back and forth, while Peter and Roscoe pulled on the anchor rope. Slowly the boat inched off the mud and concrete and then floated gracefully away from the lighthouse.

"I reckon we've used up our nine lives," Sam said.

The next five days voyage towards Crotone on the west coast of Italy was the ultimate mix of weather patterns. The wind varied from a slight breeze to a force 5, speed from one knot to 15 and they encountered huge, ugly squalls and a violent rain storm. The highlight was a nonstop 'wild fire' lightening display over the Ionian Sea which lit up the sky covering a 180° arc over the horizon for 20 or so minutes.

During the sail, navigator Sam attempted to take a mid-day sighting with the plastic sextant.

"You prick. You don't have a watch, Sam. To take a mid-day sight, you must know the exact time of Greenwich, better known as Greenwich Mean Time," explained Peter peering over Sam's shoulder.

"Only Roscoe has a watch. What if his watch is fast or slow? It still would be wrong," replied Sam.

"Give it away, Sam. I can't see the point in taking a sighting."

"Yeah, but the sextant has been lying around all trip. It's nice to at least have a go."

Crotone was reached without further incident and was spent stocking up with stores, drinking at a local café, hunting out shackles and hanks for the boat and celebrating Anchor's birthday.

Anchor, feeling guilty about the money squandered on the various cowboy marine mechanics sought out a local to fix the starter motor that had now completely failed.

"You fix. I only pay when it works," he ordered yet again.

Returning it the same day the mechanic re-fixed it in the engine, "That will be 52,000 lira please," he said.

"No, you get motor to start."

The oil was changed and the mechanic fiddled with the motor. Eventually he managed to get the motor to start, but a loud banging noise began and the whole engine began vibrating.

"You bloody Italian Cockroach," yelled Anchor. "Get the hell out of here." The mechanic left, swearing and gesturing his way along the quay.

"I reckon the motor's fucked. It's cost us a bloody fortune," said Peter, in the understatement of the year.

After two days Sam began peering at the school atlas. "Let's head for Sicily."

So with a 5–8 knot easterly wind blowing, *Antipodean* left Crotone. Progress was slow and then *Antipodean* became becalmed.

Anchor's birthday celebrations continued. Five litres of cheap wine and a bottle of duty free scotch, slipped down nicely and soon everyone on board was the worse for wear. Twice Roscoe fell overboard and *Antipodean* left to her own devices nearly colliding with a big cabin cruiser.

The next day at 9.00am Saturday 12 October, the sails were raised. With the wind coming up from the south, the yacht was pushed along nicely towards the bottom of the shoe of Italy. Suddenly after about an hour, the shackle at the top of the genoa connecting it to the halyard disintegrated, sending it crashing down onto the deck.

"Your turn to take the bosons chair and bring it down," ordered Kaffir looking at Roscoe.

Without complaining Roscoe was hoisted up and the halyard returned, but there was another dose of similar drama the following morning.

In the early hours, the wind picked up to around 33 knots and heavy seas began buffeting the boat. The wind and big seas caused the genoa halyard to tangle with the jib halyard and both ended up wrapped firmly around the mast.

"It's your turn now, Anchor," said Kaffir, issuing the same order.

Ignoring the big swell Anchor climbed up to the top of the mast as the yacht rolled in the swell. Everyone held their collective breaths as Anchor delicately managed to untangle the sails often by holding on to the mast with one hand.

"That was a pretty brave thing to do," complimented Kaffir slapping Anchor on the back when he returned to deck.

"Reminds me of Peter's sighting of Grot when he was washed overboard between Tunis and Pantelleria."

"You guys have got guts."

Relative calm returned so, the next day Roscoe went up the mast to free and tie the jib halyard so it wouldn't jam again. Sam set about mending the tears in the jib and main sail, while the others lamented the fact that progress was slow and they were still 25 miles from Messina, the gateway port of Sicily.

For the next three days, the weather continued its unpredictable pattern. A south westerly pushed them along at 4 knots through the Straits of Messina which separates Sicily from the Italian mainland. Then it dropped. It was replaced by a gusting rain storm that lasted for 12 hours. Just as it began to abate a force 7 wound up from the west, blowing them from the Straits to 30 miles north of Sicily.

It was a battle against the high waves with their long overhanging crests. It was now a force 9. Sheets of foam continually came at them in dense white streaks. The sea took on a white appearance and visibility drifted from zero to about 100 feet.

"This is getting serious. There's little food left and we've run out of water," said Roscoe after doing a quick stocktake of stores.

"We'll sit it out and then tack our way back to the Straits in the morning, seek shelter and then use the currents to make Messina," Captain Kaffir replied.

"To think people pay to go sailing. What a wank," added Roscoe.

It was a long testing day and night but daylight saw a wind change and the storm abate. By mid-afternoon, a tail wind pushed *Antipodean* back into the Straits and at last she found shelter. Nothing much was said that day. When night fall came, they fell into their bunks totally exhausted.

With no water or food, the crew were a sorry sight. Dirty, unshaven with uncouth beards and long oily hair, it was not a good look when eventually; the motor was started for the three-mile trip into port.

"I'm not sure we'll make it into port under motor," said Peter, eyeing the black smoke billowing throughout the cabin.

"It's knocking again. I tell you it's fucked."

Antipodean eventually limped into Messina. From the yacht they could see Europe's tallest volcano Mt Etna in the background but that was the furthest thing on their minds as they headed to the nearest bar for food and drink. It was agreed that the next day be spent provisioning the boat and undertaking repairs before heading for Sardinia.

"We'll replace the motor when we find a civilised place," said Anchor. "We can't get across the Pacific the way it is," he said in another gross understatement.

"It's market day so let's get cracking," said Sam.

The shopping expedition to the nearby market caused lots of commotion. They refused to buy anything without trying first. The locals crowded around.

"Are you in television?" asked one small boy addressing Anchor who looked like a working man's version of Charles Manson.

"Yes, I'm Jesus Christ and I've come to save the world again." The small boy looked on in amazement before his mother ushered him between the stalls.

"Stop touching me," Anchor growled, shoving away an old woman. This was not a good move as a group of men appeared out of nowhere, yelling and getting aggressive.

"Shit, it's time we scarpered. We've spent £40. It's busted the kitty. It's the most expensive market that's put up with us," said Sam. They trudged back to the boat.

Following the Captain's orders, the rest of the Saturday was spent on the boat. Sam, Peter and Anchor mended the genoa and mizzen. Kaffir and Roscoe went ashore to buy metal brackets to secure the main mast while Anchor assembled a tent over his bunk to stop sea water dripping onto his bed.

A visit to the marina shower and laundry facilities refreshed them and what was left of the day was spent resting.

In the morning, everyone was up bright and early praying that the winds would be kind to them.

"We'll have to manoeuvre out of our mooring under sail. I don't trust the motor," said Kaffir. "It's going to be tricky with all the boats and ships around so take it easy."

For a change everything went according to plan and making 3–4 knots under jib and headsail; they were safely out of the Straits of Messina, heading north-west towards Sardinia.

But, 74 miles out into the Tyrrhenian Sea, a wind sprung up from the west in the direction they wanted to go. It gradually increased during the day and early evening and by 3 o'clock in the morning became a force 9 gale. The seas started to swell. Soon, high 8 feet waves loomed over *Antipodean* and dense streaks of foam and water soared off the crests, smothered the deck and filled the cockpit. The blowing spray reduced visibility.

Hanging grimly to the boat rail, Kaffir sensed trouble. Big trouble!

Meanwhile Lazzaro Varriano had just finished his night shift as a security officer at All'aeroporto di Lamezia tucked away on the south west shoe of Italy. His job, from dawn to dusk six days a week, was to patrol the various out buildings and sheds that housed the heavy equipment needed to construct a new airport, the largest project ever undertaken in the Calabria region of Italy.

But this night was particularly slow. The continuous driving rain had confined him to a cramped tin shed which also doubled as a make shift canteen. The coffee was lukewarm and the air stank of stale Nazionali cigarette smoke. He was bored and tired.

Lazzaro reflected on how lucky he was to work on this historic project. The 18-year-old travelled each day from Pizzo some 11 miles away to earn money to feed his ageing parents and two younger brothers. His family were again eating healthy food and laughter and stories buzzed around the kitchen table.

He stuck his head outside the shed. It was 9.30am and he was looking forward to seeing his family and grabbing some sleep. Throwing a jacket over his head he began to run towards his motor cycle. The rain was pelting down, made worse by a howling gale which whipped along the coastline and buffeted the new exposed airport site which jutted out onto the Mediterranean Sea.

Just as he was about to rev up his bike he heard a muffled voice.

"Help – come quick! There's trouble out to sea," the voice yelled above the wind.

It was a fisherman who had been down to the nearby beach to check his small clinker built fishing boat which was anchored off shore.

"What do you mean trouble?" asked Lazzaro approaching the man.

"I've seen two distress flares. I think there are two boats in desperate trouble in this storm just off the coast. If they come close to shore they won't survive."

"Where did you see the flares?"

"I saw one about two miles away and the other, ohhh about another two miles away. I'm not sure of the distance, but I tell you there are boats in trouble out there."

Lazzaro was tired. *Maybe the flares were flashes of lightening which continually lit the sky. What if there were no ships in danger*, he thought. The fisherman persevered.

"Please come. No one will survive out there."

"Wait," said Lazzaro. "I'll get some wet weather gear and we'll go."

The two of them set off down a twisting stone path to the beach that spanned 310 miles of coastline. Bracing against the howling wind and sea spray, they threaded their way along the foreshore. Progress was slow as they trudged along in silence for about 45 minutes.

The early morning sky was grey and visibility in the conditions was limited. Then Lazzaro saw it. Away in the distance the shell of a boat was floundering among the waves about 75 yards off shore.

"You're right. There's been a disaster," he said as the two of them broke into a jog.

The next few hours were to be ones he would never forget.

Wind gusts up to 45 knots and heavy seas continued to buffet and smash high over the yacht, which was heaving wildly out of control. For the first time on the sea, the crew experienced their first knockdown (Where the mast goes below horizontal and into the sea). By 9.00am, both the jib and mizzen were lost and the tiller was swinging wildly out of control. The crew were hanging on for dear life.

"I can't handle the tiller," Sam's muffled voice rang out.

"Lash it down," replied Kaffir, panic stricken. "We'll have to ride this out."

The wind continued to buffer the yacht with increased ferocity.

"Kaffir, shit, we're being blown to the north east, away from Sardinia. It will dump us on the Italian coast," uttered Roscoe. A lump filled Kaffir's throat. He gulped.

The cabin was totally flooded as waves continued to crash inside. Nothing on board was dry. Kaffir gathered everyone around him in a huddle inside the flooded cockpit.

"Look, the boat won't break up so long as we can keep her out to sea. She's a tough old girl. It's imperative we try and keep away from the Italian coast. No sleep for anyone for 24 hours."

Tuesday 22 October, 1974 was no different. The storm continued to batter the helpless yacht as it floundered out of control. No one slept and there was urgency in every spoken word. It was 2.00am.

"Anchor, Peter. You guys keep bailing the cabin. I'm worried that those twinkling lights in the distance are houses on the coast. I'll try and turn her about and head south and hope there's a bay somewhere where we can shelter," yelled Captain Kaffir above the wind.

For the next three hours, nothing changed as *Antipodean* careered out of control in the 30-foot swells. The lights along the coast became clearer as the yacht was swept closer. Another meeting was held.

"I don't think we're going to make it. I'm going to set off that emergency flare that old guy gave us in Greenwich. It's the same type I set off in Gibraltar so I hope the fuck it works okay this time. Anchor, gather all our valuables and the boat's paperwork and stuff and seal them in that 20 litre plastic drum. Sam, you're the best swimmer. Put the traveller's cheques and all our passports in plastic and stuff them inside your Speedos," said Kaffir. Everyone felt numb.

The flare was eventually clumsily assembled and after four or five attempts finally lit. Fluorescent coloured streaks temporarily hung in the sky and were then quickly whisked away by the wind.

"Roscoe, find what clothes you can and pack them into the sail bags. Then secure a fender to each bag so they can float to shore," said the distraught captain, trying to be as calm as possible.

The yacht was a hive of activity and there was light banter among the crew. They somehow knew that worse was to come.

"Let's all meet in four days' time at Trafalgar Square," Roscoe joked, "and carry a copy of The Financial Times."

The Italian coast was now only about a mile away and as daybreak opened up, the only thing to be seen in the distance were white breakers which smashed onto the beach.

"I've stacked the life jackets over there," said Peter, pointing the corner of the cockpit.

"They're probably useless like everything else," responded Kaffir. "I think we may be in luck. It looks like a sandy beach 'cause the waves are breaking together in a line. There doesn't appear to be any rocks." he said squinting towards the shoreline.

"Why are cats soft and fluffy?" asked Roscoe. "Because they don't hurt your foot when you kick 'em." Everyone laughed.

"I've got a couple," said Peter.

"I went to buy some camouflage trousers the other day but I couldn't find any."

"Did you hear about the Police arresting two kids yesterday? One was drinking battery acid, the other was eating fireworks. They charged one and let the other one off."

No one laughed. Tension was rising.

By 7.00am, Antipodean was about 800 yards from shore but still floundering side on to the waves. She was rocking vigorously to and fro, entirely at the mercy of the wind and sea. Foam and spay dominated visibility.

They were in about 60ft of water so Kaffir and Peter decided to drop anchor to stabilise the yacht. Anchor announced he was going below to have his last crap on the boat. A nervous one!

Then in quick succession two huge waves struck. It tossed the boat onto its side, smashing the main mast and sending the crew careering into the wild and unpredictable sea.

The first wave dragged Kaffir underneath the overturned boat and carried him along under it. Sam was still in the cabin and as the yacht toppled, he was temporarily in darkness. As the super structure broke away from the hull there was an avenue of light. Sam scrambled towards the light and dived into the sea.

Roscoe rushed to the stern and dived into the second wave bearing down on the yacht just as the cabin disintegrated. A few yards away, Peter floated past. He was struggling under the weight of the three jumpers he was wearing and injuries he sustained being swept across the deck. Nursing a deep gash on his shin, a cut to his head and hands and a badly bruised back he was in serious trouble.

As the swell dipped, Roscoe spotted a fender and with great effort eventually grabbed it and struggling, paddled to Peter who gratefully accepted and clung to the old car tyre for all he was worth. Roscoe let the waves carry him to shore.

Kaffir who was the first to leave the boat, managed to extricate himself from under the yacht and was busy trying to tread water, his head bobbing under and above the water. His clothes weighed him down making it difficult to assess the situation.

"I'm not fuckin' drowning here," he yelled. Nobody heard him.

He saw Peter who was obviously concerned about his captain. "Are you okay?" Peter screamed at him.

"Yeah, don't worry about me. There are more waves coming. You just ride the swell with the fender to shore."

Between him and the beach he could see the wreck of *Antipodean* breaking up in front of his eyes. The main structure was now semi submerged and rolling in the surf.

Kaffir fought to remove the greatcoat but every time he tried, the sea would drag him underwater. Thrashing about three or four waves broke over him, before he finally struggled out of it and watched his prized possession float away. Gasping for air he saw the boat's hatch floating by. Exhausted, he grabbed it and used it to let the waves and surf carry him to shore. Stumbling out of the water he collapsed onto the beach.

Meanwhile Sam came up for air and knowing it would be dangerous to swim to shore, partially shed his clothes and swam away from the disintegrating yacht to avoid the debris. Being an accomplished surfer and swimmer and clad only in his Speedos he surveyed the scene. To his right, he could see Anchor who was naked and trying to keep his head above water. Using the incoming waves Sam managed to manoeuvre across to him.

He grabbed Anchor's hand and together they began to float on their backs.

"Look, we'll be fine. Don't panic. Be calm. Don't talk. Don't fight against the sea. Just let the current and waves do the work. There's only one way they are going and that's to shore," Sam said gasping.

Gradually, they worked their way to shore and saw Kaffir discard the hatch and stumble onto the beach.

Within 50 yards of the beach, in short breaths Sam instructed Anchor how to body surf the breakers.

"Get on the back of the wave and let it run its course. Then wait for the next and repeat. I'll be behind you and keep an eye on you. Off you go."

It took what seemed an eternity before the two of them staggered and then finally stumbled out of the surf and collapsed onto the sand.

Anchor lay motionless on the beach as the rain whipped his face. Roscoe and Kaffir were safe too but stunned and in shock. Sam looked out to sea and saw Peter coming in but at the ocean's mercy. He waded out into the undertow and yelled, "try and ride the waves!" His voice just didn't carry. Peter was distressed, fatigued and had no energy left. He had also lost the fender that Roscoe had passed to him.

He came closer and just as Sam was about to dive into the sea to rescue him, the super structure of the yacht loomed up beside Peter riding the wave. In an instant, the downward pressure of the surf picked up the boats shell and hurled it high into the air.

"Shit, it's going to land on him," Sam screamed to nobody in particular.

The shell of the yacht weighing at least a ton, smashed back down into the sea missing Peter by just a couple of yards from where he was floundering in the water. The wash flung him sideways.

Sam waded out and with an arm around him lurched and half carried his mate through the undertow to shore.

They both lay on the beach breathless.

"Shit, Peter, you nearly drowned out there," Sam said.

Peter was too exhausted to respond.

Not a word was spoken as the five of them lay on the beach recovering, lucky to be alive. The only sounds were the screeching wind, the patter of rain and the echo of the surf breaking onto the beach.

Eventually Kaffir sat up, "Is everyone okay?"

"No, I feel like shit," responded Anchor.

"Shit happens and now we've lost our home," Kaffir said.

Slowly everyone started to move, gradually rising to their feet and then flexing their muscles attempting to be brave under the circumstances. Dazed and in shock, Peter and Anchor gazed out to sea.

"We nearly died out there," Anchor muttered to Peter. "I'm never going to have a crap on a boat again," he vowed.

The next few hours were spent walking gingerly back and forth along the shore line gathering their gear. All the heavy sail bags, other belongings and the 20 litre plastic container were found, dragged and stacked above the high tide line. Roscoe opened one, found his camera and busily took photos for posterity not knowing the film was ruined.

The only remnants from the wreck on the beach were the cabin structure and unrecognisable debris.

"What do we do now? Where the hell are we, Sam?"

"I've got no bloody idea," answered navigator Sam. "We'll have to go for help," he said, shivering still clad in only his Speedos.

They began to walk wearily along the beach in relative silence towards a headland about two miles away. Deep in thought, Kaffir finally broke the silence, "You know, if we had had decent charts we could have run in to the corner of a bay and found a little fishing port. The only chart we had was the one we pinched in Pireaus. It covered an area from Gibraltar to Greece, about 2000 miles. The scale of the chart was massive, so there was no detail. Plenty of sea and land masses though," he mumbled.

No one spoke a word. There was a strong silence.

After about 20 minutes, they saw two men jogging towards them. As they got closer they began babbling in Italian.

"*Non comprehendo*," said Roscoe. "We speak only Englise."

"My name Lazzaro. Who are you?" one of the Italians replied in broken English.

"We're Aussies and Kiwis. We were going to sail our yacht across the Pacific to Australia, but now it's shipwrecked," Roscoe said.

"Come to airport. We dry you off."

The seven of them with heads bowed into the howling wind trudged along the water's edge. Nothing was said as everyone was too exhausted and in various stages of shock. Occasionally, they all stopped and looked back keeping their thoughts private.

Eventually, they reached a construction site and were soon inside the canteen, surrounded by workers preparing for their shift, all babbling over each other in Italian. By now the storm had really taken hold and knocked out the power. They gratefully accepted cold coffee and just looked at each other not sure of the next move.

"Where the hell are we?" moaned Sam.

Lazzaro took control relishing his new found importance.

"You sank in the Golfo di Santa Eufemia. We build new airport. It called Lamezia Terme airport. I take you to San Pietro, Lametino. It's nearest village about four kilometres away. There you have drink and food at Bar Michelangelo. It where we work and we are at what will be Lamezia Terme airport. I take you to San Pietro, Lametino. It nearest village about four kilometre away. There, you have drink and food at Bar Michelangelo. It's where we meet after work," he said.

"I arrange ambulance from Lamezia. It 13kms from San Pietro. You are in the Catanzaro Province in Calabria Region."

"Yeah, but where are we?" Sam repeated.

"On coast of south-west Italy."

Sam nodded, still stunned by the experience, "Oh, shit."

After a while the crew along with some of the remaining workers ready to wind down after night shift, crammed into an old workers' transit van and were on their way to the Bar Michelangelo. The short journey was spent in silence.

The author visiting the bar Michelangelo

Bar Michelangelo was a bar that doubled as a general store. It had an alcove which stocked fruit and vegetables. A lot of empty spirit bottles lined a shelf behind an old wooden counter. It certainly was the meeting place for all the locals. Outside were plastic tables and chairs sheltered by colourful umbrellas.

The storm had knocked out the power for the whole area and without lights the bar was illuminated with candles dotted around its interior. Lazzaro continued babbling in Italian but the crew looked blankly on. Then he produced a bottle of bourbon which was gratefully accepted and shared.

Word spread fast about the village's new visitors. Some brought in towels, others clothes. Food was brought in. There was much excitement in the crowed bar. Discussion ranged from the shipwreck to demanding when power would be restored. The crew knew they were lucky to be alive. In the distance the wailing of a siren could be heard approaching the bar.

"Ambulance on way," Lazzaro said. "It take you to Lamezia Terme hospital so you can be checked out."

After handshakes and hugs all-round, the five of them crammed into the rear of the ambulance. With its siren blaring it headed to the hospital, a trip that took less than 15 minutes.

The driver was taking no prisoners and sped off dodging traffic along its way. Approaching a round-about without slowing, he braked suddenly to avoid a car. Within a split second he collided with a moped, sending the occupant spiralling in the air and onto the roadway. Peter thumped on the small glass pane which separated the driver from the others.

"Hey, you've caused a crash. Stop and help him." The orderly with them in the back looked blankly on. "He's not going to stop. This is bloody awful."

Arriving at the hospital, Peter did not let up. "What about the bloke on the scooter? Are you going back for him?" The driver and the orderly who could not speak or understand English showed no interest in the conversation.

Orderlies ran out with stretchers, "We're okay to walk," offered Anchor.

The five on them limped into the hospital and without paperwork were led to a six-room ward painted in blue and red and decorated with motifs depicting humpty dumpty, and other childish cartoon characters.

"Jeez, I reckon this is the maternity hospital. Doesn't 'l'ospedale di maternità' mean maternity? Look at all those Sheilas with babies opposite. Christ, what next?" whispered Roscoe.

Being foreigners the crew got the royal treatment. Within the hour, Peter had stitches in his shin and everyone had anti-tetanus injections in their backsides.

All slept peacefully that night.

In the morning they began discussing their next move. The conversation was broken when a nurse came into the ward.

"There are some people to see you," she said. "Who is your leader?"

"That's me," answered Kaffir.

It was mid-afternoon, when two naval police officers and a representative from the Port Authority and an interpreter began questioning Kaffir in the hospital superintendent's office. "Who are you?" asked an officer.

"We were sailing our yacht when we struck a storm," replied Kaffir. Producing a large chart the officer said, "Where did you come ashore?"

Peering at the chart for a long time, it was difficult for Kaffir to get his bearings.

"About there," said Kaffir pointing to the coast line on the chart.

"Where did you come from? What do you all do?"

"We do nothing. We are sailors preparing to sail our yacht across the Pacific." The naval police looked at each other.

"We don't believe you. Look at you. You're hippies. You're drug runners."

"No. No Sir."

"You didn't come ashore where you claim. It was about 20 miles away."

"No, it was about there," said Kaffir nervously again studying and then pointing to the chart. The three officers left the room leaving him alone.

About half an hour later, they returned with a new chart and asked Kaffir again, "Where did you come ashore? Who are you? Where did you come from?" they repeated. Kaffir gave the same answers. The onlookers were not convinced and again left the room. *Shit*, thought Kaffir, *what the hell's going on?*" He sat gathering his thoughts.

An hour later, they returned with yet another fresh chart and went through all the questions again. Kaffir was being thoroughly interrogated. All through this one officer continually made notes of the responses and reviewed them after each question and session. The questioning went on for two hours.

When they returned for the third time the interrogating officer told Kaffir that they had seen a distress flare about 20 miles away and had sent up a helicopter to investigate and search.

"We don't like sending out our air rescue squad at 4.30 in the morning," he said.

"But I told you, we sent up a flare at about 7.30 in the morning, not 4.30 and we were shipwrecked there," responded Kaffir again pointing to the chart. The Port Authority representative was getting restless.

"My job is to accurately pin point wrecks and advise the authority so they can be added to the international shipwreck charts. We found lots of debris a long way from there."

"Well, then it must have been another boat," replied Kaffir.

"Wait here and don't leave the hospital. A colleague is bringing some photos of the wreck for you to look at.

At around 9.00pm, they all convened again with a new face in attendance.

"I'm Otto, head of the local Port Authority," he said introducing himself. "I want to help you the best I can and these gentlemen have some photos to show you. Do you recognise anything in these pictures or of this wreck?" he asked showing Kaffir a series of photos.

There was an air of expectancy in the room.

"No, I don't recognise anything. That's not our boat.

Otto turned to the others.

"Then, I confirm that the wreck is of another boat a couple of hours earlier. It was owned by two Americans that drowned."

There was silence.

"But how do you know this?" one asked.

"For identification purposes, all harbours along the coast were advised of the sad news this morning. Two bodies have been found on the beach. That's why I'm here."

While Kaffir had spent most of the day persuading the authorities they were not drug runners and had told the truth for a change, the others were having their own experience of Italian hospitality.

First it was a hot shower and then, one by one, a visit to the hospital hairdresser for a wash, cut and blow dry. The afros all came up a treat. The beards were washed and trimmed into a decent shape.

"You look quite sexy Sam with all that hair puffed up," said Peter teasing him.

"You don't look so bad yourself. Actually, I don't quite recognise you."

The four of them were then issued with starched stiff pyjamas and regulation hospital slippers and ushered back into their ward.

"This will look pretty dodgy on a postcard. Four blokes in a hospital maternity ward waiting to give birth," Roscoe joked.

Sitting up in bed, everyone began to cheer up realising that they were grateful to be alive, even if their dream of sailing home was now doomed. After dozing for a couple of hours they were given a huge plate of spaghetti. "This is bloody good. I think I will book in here," said Anchor, ignoring the obvious sounds of babies crying down the corridor.

Then an Italian orderly came into the ward. "I've just heard about you guys," he said in a broken Australian accent. "I've lived in Aussie and I reckon you would prefer something to remind you of home. You don't want this sort of tucker. How about bacon and eggs for dinner?"

"Yeah, that would be great," they answered almost in chorus.

True to his word at 6.00pm, a possession of nurses carrying trays entered the ward.

The four of them gratefully tucked in to a huge plate of bacon, eggs and chips.

"Christ, this is the best food since we left Greece," said Peter.

"Criticising my food again?" replied Roscoe with a wide smile.

"Kaffir will be pissed off missing out on this. Great that he was elected Captain eh," remarked Sam.

"We'll sleep well tonight.

The next morning as everyone was relaxing another official immaculately dress in an Italian suit, shirt and floral tie strode into the ward.

"Let me introduce myself. I'm Patrick Flynn from the Australian Embassy in Rome. Fortunately, I was in Sparta on business and was alerted that there had been a couple of wrecks out there," he said, waving his hand towards the direction of the ocean.

"Are you alright?"

"Yeah, I think so. Our pride has been hurt though. We're very grateful for all this Italian hospitality. They've been marvellous," answered Roscoe.

"That's good. Do you have any clothes?"

Anchor described how the locals had rallied round and provided adequate clothing, albeit of various sizes and in some cases, ill fitting.

"Humm, I can't really help you there. They will have to do at the moment though.

"What about your passports?"

"They're down in my crutch. I mean had them in plastic stored there when I abandoned the yacht. It was bloody uncomfortable. Lucky Speedos are very tight fitting so they survived."

"Let me have a look."

Sam handed over the very damp passports with some pages stuck together, others with the blue ink from stamps running down the pages.

"I'll take care of these and get them replaced or over stamped with our 'international approval authorisation'," replied Patrick. "I will leave them with the hospital superintendent."

The questions and answers continued and were eventually broken when the local TV arrived with other journalists in tow.

"I'll leave you. I'm going to see your Captain, Mr Muir whom I'm told has a few problems."

The journalists began firing questions in Italian. "Hold on, hold on. Do any of you guys speak any English?" asked Roscoe taking charge.

It was to be a long interview which eventually was the lead television story throughout Italy. Their narrow escape in the storm was published on the front page of most daily newspapers along with the loss of life of the other sailors further down the coast.

Eventually they settled down for a night's sleep which was continually broken with the sounds of women giving birth in the nearby delivery room.

"These Italian women can sure make a racket," said Anchor in the morning. The others nodded, but refreshed after a good night's sleep between the sheets.

"I slept like a log too," said Kaffir who had eventually joined them late the previous evening. "Boy, did I get a grilling yesterday. Let's rest up one more day and then get out of here. I've made arrangements with the police to take us back to the beach to collect our gear."

Early the following day, the five of them went to the nurses' station and thanked those on duty.

"You guys have been great. Please thank the others," said Peter, determined to leave a good impression.

"We will drop by later and pick up our passports. Thanks," said Peter.

The police driver who picked them up came straight to the point. "You know what? There'll be nothing left on the beach." Within an hour, they arrived at the scene. They stood in silence.

The author visits the beach where Antipodean sank

"The bastards! Everything's been knocked off by the locals. They've even unbolted the anchor winch off the front of the bow section that was lying over there," said Kaffir, pointing to a tangled mess of wood and iron.

"That 80 year old huge anchor has been unbolted too. It was rusted old shit and never worked or toiled the sea," added Peter. The only thing left of *Antipodean* was the cabin structure that was sitting up all alone.

"The keel would have taken the hull straight to the bottom of the ocean. Let's not worry about the sail bags and stuff attached to the fenders. It will be like talking to a block of wood to try and find out who's knocked everything off."

"I feel sick. Let's get the hell out of here," he said, fighting back tears. "I'm meant to be having another meeting with the naval people this morning to finalise the sinking location, but they can all get stuffed. She was never registered anyway, so it would be illegal to have her registered as a sunken vessel. I don't need the hassles. We'll pick up our passports and fuck off."

"I do have some good news," said Sam. "The bloke from the Embassy has lent us £44.00. Patrick said he would give us more, but that was all the rule book would allow. He says we will have enough for a third class rail fare to Rome and what's left can be put towards the airfares to London. I will donate the last of my travellers' cheques which thank goodness have now dried out to top up the tickets."

"Now that's what I call a master plan," said Kaffir beaming, "and any dough left over can be spent having a few beers after everything is booked."

The journey to Rome and then London was uneventful and quick. On arrival, approaching the customs booth Sam said, "This is ridiculous. Here we are with no luggage, only the clothes we were given or wore when the boat sank, no money and prancing around in bloody hospital slippers." Everyone laughed.

"It's no laughing matter. The more money you have the longer you can stay in England," Roscoe said. "I had £500 when I arrived and was allowed six months," he said as they queued up.

They crowded around the customs booth. The officer eyed them carefully.

"How much money does each of you have?"

"Nothing."

Give me your passports. Ahhh, I've read about you boys. I know where you've come from. You've had quite a time eh? How long do you want?"

"We need about three months to get sorted," replied Sam.

"No problem. I'll give you 12 months," said the customs officer stamping the passports.

"Bugger me! These Poms are unreal. No money and another 12 months in the UK."

"Who wants to sail back to the Antipodes?" asked Kaffir. "Let's find another yacht!"

He was greeted with silence.

ADDENDUM

The Survivors after the sinking speak of their time on the *Antipodean*

Il Capitano, Brian Muir

"I think that I could sum up the whole experience really by saying it was the sense of achievement that you get by doing what we did. All the survival stuff that we went through, it was the mateship and the solidarity that comes out of it. We were a pretty tight bunch of mates and still are. In London they couldn't separate us for a while – they used to call us 'The Admirals'. You forget the bad times and there were lots, many more bad times, than there were good times. You just remember those fun times. Like when we were anchored up, safely in port, chasing members of the opposite sex and drinking too much alcohol! I think that stays with you forever – that's comradeship."

Sam Syme

It was my brush with death that made me realise the importance of living. The storm that Kiwi Ted and I battled with between Majorca and Gibraltar with the two Pommies, who knew nothing about sailing, was knocking on death's door. I can still visualise the boat nose diving into the ocean and the waves cascading into the cabin. I thought to myself we're having trouble here and it's going to be touch and go. So we all pulled together. It was instinctive I guess. How we survived, I'll never know. The trip was full of incidents, but in the end, camaraderie was the winner…as well as the sea."

Peter Robertson

"I can't help feeling we were just a lot of yobbos, but man, what a fantastic time we had. The bond we had grew and grew and the memories will be with me forever. What a shame the *Antipodean* died the way she did. It will never leave the sea and the mysteries and surprises it will throw up."

Quentin Rvan

"One thing for sure, I will not use the loo in the teeth of a storm ever again! I am grateful that Kaffir and the boys gave me the opportunity to share such and adventure. *Antipodean* was a lovely lady, but I reckon she deserved a better crew and fate. The experience enriched my life."

Ross Seward

"What a pleasure to be the resident cook and be part of such an unruly lot. It's amazing when you reflect on what we got up to. You wouldn't get away with it today, that's for sure. I really enjoyed my time on *Antipodean*, but every dream has to end. To have my life still intact after the near drowning experience at the end, has given me a new sense of living and what it means.

This book has come about after four reunions over a period of 14 years when each segment of the journey was discussed, recorded and transcribed.

In addition reference was also made to a water stained ships log maintained by Roscoe from the time he arrived in Gibraltar until the sinking.

To commemorate the 20th anniversary of the sinking, a reunion of all those who were associated with the yacht was held in October 1994.

THE END